ADVANCING

WordPerfect

Carol McKenzie
Pat Tidswell

HEINEMANN
EDUCATIONAL

Heinemann Educational,
a division of Heinemann Publishers (Oxford) Ltd
Halley Court, Jordan Hill, Oxford OX2 8EJ

OXFORD LONDON EDINBURGH
MADRID ATHENS BOLOGNA PARIS
MELBOURNE SYDNEY AUCKLAND SINGAPORE
TOKYO IBADAN NAIROBI HARARE
GABORONE PORTSMOUTH NH (USA)

First Published 1993

97 96 95 94 93
10 9 8 7 6 5 4 3 2

A catalogue record for this book is available from the British Library on request

ISBN 0 435 451189

Designed by Ken Vail Graphic Design, Cambridge
using Quark XPress™ 3.1 on the Apple Macintosh™ Ci

Printed in Great Britain by Thomson Litho, East Kilbride, Scotland

Acknowledgements
The authors and publishers would like to thank the RSA for permission to reproduce examination requirements.

Contents

Advancing WordPerfect has been written as a continuation text to *Extending WordPerfect* and *Introducing WordPerfect** by the same authors. It has been designed as a progressive course and is suitable for use in the classroom, in an open learning workshop, or as a private study aid.

Advancing WordPerfect will help those preparing to take advanced examinations in Word Processing, using WordPerfect Versions 5.0 or 5.1. However, the book would be equally useful to those who use WordPerfect and simply wish to extend their working knowledge.

Previous experience

It is assumed that you have completed an elementary (Stage I) and intermediate (Stage II) word processing course, using WordPerfect, and are therefore familiar with conventional document layout and text processing principles and practice. It is also assumed that you are familiar with the most commonly used WordPerfect commands as outlined in the previous books, *Introducing WordPerfect* and *Extending WordPerfect.*

Format

Full instructions for the commands and functions required in the preparation of particular documents are given at the beginning of each unit, followed by practice exercises.
Consolidation practice is available after Units 3 and 6 i.e. after all the topics for each part of each syllabus have been covered.
Print-out checks are included in the book and these may be used by both students and teachers.
Handy tips are included throughout the text to suggest ways in which functions can be carried out more quickly, easily or effectively.
A **glossary of WordPerfect commands** is available for quick reference at the back of the book.

Coverage

This book is designed for those of you preparing to take the **RSA Stage III Word Processing** examination, using WordPerfect Versions 5.0 or 5.1.
Units 1, 2 and 3 cover Part 1 of the Stage III examination.
Units 4, 5 and 6 cover Part 2 of the Stage III examination.
Consolidation work is included after Units 3 and 6.

Assessment

At the end of Unit 3 you should be able to do an RSA Stage III Part 1 paper:

(a) within a *one-and-a-quarter-hour* time limit
(b) with no more than ten accuracy and seven presentation errors for a *Pass*
(c) with no more than three accuracy and three presentation errors for a *Distinction*

At the end of Unit 6 you should be able to do an RSA Stage III Part 2 paper:

(a) within a *one-and-a-quarter-hour* time limit
(b) with no more than 6 accuracy and 4 presentation errors for a *Pass*
(c) with no more than 2 accuracy and 2 presentation errors for a *Distinction*

* These publications cover the following syllabuses:
RSA Computer Literacy and Information Technology (word processing application); RSA Core Text Processing Skills (taken on a word processor); RSA Stage I Word Processing; RSA Stage II Word Processing, Parts 1 and 2.

Using on-screen menus in WordPerfect 5.1

WordPerfect 5.1 offers the facility of drop-down on-screen menus which may be successfully used by either keyboard or mouse-driven operation, in addition to, or instead of, the function keys. Instructions to access the on-screen menus, where relevant, have been included throughout the text. The appropriate mouse commands appear in boxes to the left of the page and the keyboard commands to which they relate have been highlighted for easy identification. From this point operators may choose whether to use the mouse or the keyboard.

The menu bar appears at the top of the screen as follows:

```
File | Edit | Search | Layout | Mark | Tools | Font | Graphics | Help
```

The initial one-line menu bar may be permanently displayed on screen by choosing the appropriate options under the **Shift+F1** (Setup) key.

To select an option from the on-screen menu – keyboard operation

Press: **Alt**
Type: the highlighted letter of the option required

To select an option from the on-screen menu – mouse operation

Move the mouse pointer to the option required and click the mouse button

A drop-down menu like the one on the left will appear on screen:

```
[Move (Cut)        ]
[Copy              ]
[Paste             ]
[Append            ]
--------------------
[Delete            ]
[Undelete          ]
--------------------
[Block             ]
[Select            ]
[Comment           ]
[Convert Case      ]
[Protect Block     ]
--------------------
[Switch Document   ]
[Window            ]
--------------------
[Reveal Codes      ]
```

To exit from the on-screen menu without making a selection – keyboard operation

Press: **F7** (Exit) or **F1** (Cancel)

To exit from the on-screen menu without making a selection – mouse operation

Position the mouse pointer anywhere on screen *outside* the menu box and click the mouse button.

Working through a unit

1. *When you see this symbol read all the information* before you begin.
2. *When you see this symbol carry out the exercises.*
3. Use WordPerfect's **Spellcheck** facility to check your document, but always proofread too.
4. Use WordPerfect's **View** facility to check that your document is going to be correct when it is printed.
5. *Save your work* on to your floppy disk.
6. *Call up the directory* (List Files) of your disk on to the screen and *print your work* from this directory.
7. Compare your work with the *print-out checks* at the back of the book.

N.B. *Do not delete files from your disk, you may need them later.*

Apostrophes

At Stage III, you will be expected to know when to use an apostrophe and where it should be positioned in the word to which it relates.

An apostrophe is used to show that a letter (or letters) has been left out, for example:

don't	*(do not)*	haven't	*(have not)*
she'd	*(she had)*	you're	*(you are)*

Apostrophes are also used to show possession, e.g. that something 'belongs' to someone or something:

Nicola's pen *(the pen of Nicola)*

If there is more than one 'possessor' the apostrophe goes after the 's', for example:

The students' desks *(the desks of the students)*

In speech, 'its' can mean two things: 'it is' or 'belonging to it'. An apostrophe is used only when the full phrase of 'it is' is shortened – the apostrophe shows that a letter has been missed out, for example:

It's good but the house has *its* door painted red.

Errors of agreement

This type of error will appear in the manuscript text that you are copying (and also in the text previously keyed in for other tasks). The errors will *not* be circled at Stage III – you are expected to find these errors and correct them automatically as you key in the text.

As you are keying in text you should make sure that what you are typing makes sense – 'listen' to what you are typing.

You should watch out for errors of agreement such as:

- This class of girls are irritating.
  Should be keyed in as:
  This class of girls is irritating.
  (because there is only *one* class)
  If there were more than one class you would key in:
  These classes of girls are irritating.
- The difference between the two word processing programs were demonstrated by the supervisor.
  Should be keyed in as:
  The difference between the two word processing programs was demonstrated by the supervisor.
  (because there are *two* programs but only *one* difference)

Typographical and spelling errors

The manuscript text that you copy will also contain some typographical and/or spelling errors.

Remember always to use spellcheck before you print your work!

Be careful of homophones; for example:

here	*and*	hear
their	*and*	there
course	*and*	coarse
are	*and*	our

Spellcheck will not find this type of error – it's up to you to read the text and choose the correct version.

Business letter on A4 pre-printed letterhead

One of the tasks in the RSA Stage III Part 1 examination is to *key in a business letter* and print it out *on A4 letterheaded paper.*

A letterhead has the name and address of the sender printed at the top of the sheet. Included in this book are three sample letterheads. You could photocopy these and use them for practice.

In Part 1 of the Stage III examination you can also expect to come across the following.

Complete business letter in fully blocked style

As well as the reference and date, there will be a 'special mark', e.g. URGENT, PERSONAL, and a subject heading. The complimentary close will include the name of the organisation, and the name and designation of the sender.

Enclosure and routing to be indicated

Enclosures should be indicated at the foot of the letter in the usual way.

The text will mention a copy of the letter being sent to a named person or organisation (routing).

To *indicate routing* leave at least one clear line after Enc(s) and type:

Copy to (insert name of person or organisation)

Information to be located and inserted

There are two possible sources of information to be inserted into a task:

1 another task in the examination paper

2 an announcement made by the invigilator.

(Early in the examination the invigilator will read out a piece of information that is to be incorporated into any one of the three tasks. Have a pencil handy so you can jot it down.)

Abbreviations and unfamiliar words

The RSA list of abbreviations is the same for Stage III as for Stage II.

Indented text

A section of text (typescript or manuscript) may be indented for emphasis in any of the three tasks. You should retain the indentation, even though no specific instruction is given to you.

Handy tip

'Hard' spaces between words

Sometimes, it is desirable to keep 2 words or symbols together rather than having them separated by the wraparound function.

For example, reading is made more difficult if **25 mm** is split as it is in this sentence, and also **Mr Nettleton** would be better all on one line.

To avoid this (using the above example):

Type: **25**
Press: **Home**
Press: **Spacebar**
Type: **mm**

25 mm will be kept together either at the end of the first line or at the beginning of the second line.

Handy tip

Changing the unit of measurement

If your status line shows the Line and Position indicators in inches, you can change the display. The Line display can be changed to tell you which line you are on and the Position display can be changed to show the column position in pitch.

Press: **Shift + F1** (Setup key)
Press: **8** (Units of Measure)
Press: **1** (Display)
Type: **u** (WordPerfect Units Lines/Columns)
Press: **2** (Status Line Display)
Type: **u** (WordPerfect Units Lines/Columns)
Press: **F7** (Exit)

Producing a print-out on an A4 letterhead

It is the candidate's responsibility to print out the work in both parts of the RSA Stage III examinations.

Your ability to print out this task and the method you use will depend on your printer. If you are taking an examination you will need guidance from your tutor or printer manual on:

1 **The top margin to be used on your document.**
Changing the top margin is one way of making sure that your printing starts at the correct point vertically on the printed letterhead.

2 **Feeding the paper into your printer and positioning it correctly (vertically).**
Placing the letterhead in a particular position in the printer is another way of making sure that your printing starts at the correct point.

3 **Feeding the paper into your printer and positioning it correctly (horizontally).**
The paper guide mechanism on your printer should be set so that when you print your letter, the left margin aligns as closely as possible with the printing on the letterhead.

Look at the print-out checks for Unit 1 on pages 00 to 00 and check the correct positioning of printing on a letterhead.

4 **Ensuring that the text at the bottom of your document will be printed on the letterhead.**
Some printers do not print the last few lines of a document when single sheets of paper are being used. It is important that you find a way of solving this problem if it occurs on your printer because this task is usually a long one and takes up a full page.

Note: if you are working on your own, without a tutor, you should experiment with this task to make sure that you can satisfy the requirements using your printer. Refer to your printer manual or manufacturer if you have difficulties.

1.1 **Exercise 1a.**

Remember to be aware of consistency of presentation. Key in Exercise 1a. The information to be incorporated into your letter is *Opportunities Unlimited.*

Read the following points before you begin.

Inserting your name and other details

It is usual practice in an examination to key in your name, centre number and the task number as line 1 of a document. However, when the printing is to be done on a letterhead these details are best positioned *on the same line as the date, and flush with the right margin,* for example:

12 December 1992 Your name Ex 1A

Changing 'pitch' in business letter

The letter may be a long one. You may be able to make the letter fit on one page by changing the pitch from 10 CPI to 12 CPI.

To change the pitch (or base font):

```
Font
Base Font ↵
```

1. Position the cursor at the top of your document.
2. Press: **Ctrl + F8**
3. Select: **4** (Base Font)
4. Select: **12 CPI** (move cursor to 12 CPI and press 1 to select)
5. Move to bottom of document and check that document now fits on one page. (See page 000 for more information.)

Handy tip

Automatic date format

WordPerfect can automatically insert the date for you when you press **Shift + F5** (Date/Outline). If you want to use this facility you need to set up the date format as follows:

Press: **Shift + F5**
Press: **3** (for Date Format)
Type: **1 3 4** (to choose usual format e.g. 1 January 1992)
Press: **F7** (to exit back to document)

To insert date automatically at cursor:

Press: **Shift + F5**
Press: **1** (to insert date)

Note: this function will work satisfactorily only if the current date on your computer is correctly set, and the batteries have not run out!

1.2 Exercise 1a.
continued

Save and print a copy of your work on an 'Opportunities Unlimited' A4 letterhead. Use the filename **EX1A**

Letter to Mrs A Bottomley, 26 Hollings Way, BOROUGHTON, BB10 1WB. Mark PRIVATE please. Use ragged right margin. Save as EX 1A and print a copy on an OPPORTUNITIES UNLIMITED letterhead.

USE 12 PITCH SO LETTER WILL FIT ON ONE PAGE

Dr Mrs B——

'GOING IT ALONE' SEMINAR – Sat (insert date for Sat after next)

underscore all heading

CAPS

Further to yesterdays telephone conversation, I wd like ~~to let~~ give you have more info on the above event wh is aimed at providing prospective 'entreprenuers' w the opp to acquire as much info as poss ~~in as short a time~~ as poss.

At O—— U——, we ~~are very aware of~~ ack the fact that setting up in bus on yr own is an enormous step to ~~make~~ take & ~~it is important to have details of gov and schemes wh could~~ we aim to help the budding businessman or businesswoman ~~in the~~ thro' the early stages. At the seminar, you wl be able to benefit from the knowledge and exp of local ~~traders~~ leaders of bus & industry.

The day wl begin at 9.30 am w a talk by our Director, followed by approx one hour of presentations on currant 'start-up" schemes. After coffee at 1100 hrs, the participants wl be invited to sep into small group & to pool there ideas & exps in considering what make a successfull bus. The afternoon wl be your chance to put yr idea(s) to an advisor and to rec individual advice. I enclose a map showing the location of our temp accom, & a leaflet on the seminar. I look forward to seeing you.

at the Seminar

Yrs ffly

EA SUTCLIFFE
Conference Organiser

I have sent a copy of this letter to Ms P Farren, yr colleague

1.3 **Exercise 1b.** Key in Exercise 1b, making all necessary amendments as you go along.

1.4 Save and print a copy of your work on a 'George Carter' A4 letterhead. Use the filename **EX1B**.

EX1B is to be printed on a letterhead. Please use a justified right margin. Mark the letter 'for the attention of the Health & Safety Officer'.

RETAIN 10 PITCH

A GOOD PLACE TO WORK?

The name of the factory is SEAVIEW RD

Baxter, Green & Co
Yates Quay
EASTPORT
ET4 7GH

Dr Sirs

Thank you for contacting me recently in response to our newspaper advert. // The GOOD P___ T___ W___? Campaign began in (last month) of this yr and has def recd a good response, both from employers & employees. The project employs 3 f/t workers, & approx three p/t assistants (from the region) are used at each ~~venue~~ site ✓ to ensure info reaches local orgs.

Our campaigns mobile caravan wl be in ~~yr~~ the Eastport area in (Month after next) and, as you know, we are looking for a suitable sight to locate the caravan. It is necy for us to be in the bus centre of a town w suff car parking space for people to be encouraged to visit the exhibition without incon. Yr ______ factory wd appear to be ideal and I have written to yr Managing Director, (JAMES GREEN,) requesting permission to use yr companys resources. I have send him a copy of this letter. (lower case)

I enclose a brochure giving info on the (exhibition) and (project) and hope to here from you ~~soon~~ before (a week on Friday) so that arrangments can be finalised.

Yrs ffly

H HAMILTON
Project Leader

Letter with continuation sheet

The letter may be too long to fit on one page even pitch in 12. In this case, the first page should be printed on the A4 letterheaded sheet provided and the second page should be printed on one of the sheets of A4 plain paper.

Decide on a sensible place to insert a hard page break to form page 2; this page should be numbered. Refer to the glossary for WordPerfect's methods of page numbering.

Your name and exercise number should be printed on both pages. You could use any of the following methods.

- *Method 1*: Set a *header* to print your name and exercise number at the *top right of both pages.*
- *Method 2*: Set a *footer* to print your name and exercise number at the *foot of both pages.*
- *Method 3*: Key in your name and exercise number on page 1 opposite the date as previously instructed. Key in your name etc. again at the top of page 2.

1.5 **Exercise 1c.**

Retrieve the file **EX1B** and add the following text just before the paragraph that begins 'I enclose...'

It is very important that as many people as poss visit the exhibition in view of the fact that legislation ~~comes into force very soon~~ is already in place. The E_____ C_____ guidelines set out clear responsibilities for employers and employees alike and all managers/supervisors need to be made aware of ~~their~~ the part they must play in assessing workstations. [It is, of course, no less vital that work practices are also examined with the aim of increasing efficiency and decreasing potential dangers and factors wh might promote disease and discomfort.

DISPEL

We hope to dispel some myths by giving factual information and advise based on thorough research.

(EC = European Community)

1.6 Insert your name and exercise number using one of the methods described. Set page numbering, suppressing this feature on page 1. Insert a hard page break in a sensible place.

1.7 Save and print a copy of your work. Use the filename **EX1C.**

Summary of requirements

In this Unit, and in Unit 3, you will practise all the text editing techniques you have previously learned.

This task in the RSA Stage III Part 1 examination is to be keyed in and can test any (or all) or the items from the following list:

ragged/justified right margin
change of line spacing within a document
insetting/indenting of text
consistency of presentation
errors of agreement
typographical errors
apostrophes
manuscript correction signs
changing of line length
abbreviations
moving blocks of text

Refresh your memory on all of these topics before you begin.

Points to remember

1. It is easier to set a header to show your name, centre number and task number on each page when a document takes up more than one page.
2. Multi-page documents should usually have pages numbered – but not the first page.
3. You should insert page breaks in sensible places.
4. Follow the usual procedures for making sure that your work is completely accurate – proofread very carefully, spellcheck and view before printing.

> ## *Handy tip*
> ### Inserting accents on foreign words
> If your printer will support accents and they are available on your keyboard, you can use the compose function to produce a *composite character*, e.g. the â in 'pâtisserie'.
>
> *Before* typing the character:
>
> Press: **Ctrl** + **2** (number 2 *not* **F2**)
> Type: **a** (or required letter)
> Type: ^ (the circumflex or other accent)

> ## *Handy tip*
> To enter a in WordPerfect:
> Press: **Alt** + **171**
>
> To enter c in WordPerfect:
> Press: **Alt** + **172**
>
> (*Note*: although the fractions appear on screen, your printer type will determine whether or not they will print out.)

Handy tip

To edit a header or footer

If you wish to change the format or content of a header, it is not necessary to delete the command and start again – you can edit the header you have set.

To edit a header:

Press: **Shift** + **F8**
Press: **2** (Page)
Press: **3** (Headers)
Press: **1** (Header A)
Press: **5** (Edit)
Make the required formatting changes
Press: **F7** (Exit)

To edit a footer, press **4** (Footers) at the **Page Format** menu.

Layout
Page

Exercise 2a.

Exercise 2A (This leaflet draft is based on Exercise 1A. Refer to that task for any information you need)

(Ragged margin please)

G___ I___ A___ SEMINAR
(2 clear lines)
Saturday (insert date)
} centre & underline

Opportunities Unlimited are ~~proud~~ pleased to ~~announce~~ organise this Seminar for prospective business owners in the Boroughton area.

The Seminar will be held in the ground floor function suite and the programme for the day has been organized as follows:

Our offices are to be relocated ~~to~~ in the West End Business Park, where our new, ~~luxurious~~, purpose-built accommodation is nearing ~~completion~~ its end. In the meantime, we are fortunte that we have been allowed to use the premises of the ~~Stratton~~ Vendôme Hotel, High Street, for ~~the~~ our Seminar. (double spacing ✓)

Introduction – 0900 hrs (Caps & underline)

Neil Ross, Marketing Director of O___ U___ will ~~give an~~ outline the programe for the day & wl introduce the speakers and (reps) in full from local industry, business & commerce.

1000 – Start-up Schemes

Presentations will be ~~presented~~ made by the High Street banks, the Small Bus Advisory Service & the British Franchise Association.

Topics will include: capital, loans, share issues, gov schemes and development boards

Exercise 2a.

continued

1115 am – What makes an Entrepreneur?

W the aid of case ~~studies~~ histories, participants wl be encourage to ~~talk about~~ discuss the viability of the respective businesses, types of bus organisation, market research, franchising and employment law. The leader of each group wl advice on Income Tax, VAT & National Insurance. The aims is to make the participants more aware of the ~~many~~ pitfalls & pleasures of self-employment.

1100 hrs – Coffee

12.45 pm – Lunch in Carvery (1st floor)

1400 hrs – Consultation ~~&Advice~~ Sessions

The 'experts' wl make themselves available for individuel consultation. Every participant can put his/her idea foreward and rec valuable assistance.

1600 hrs – PLENARY SESSION/PRIZE PRESENTATION

N__ R__, Marketing D__, will ~~present~~ give ✓ an award – '__________' – together w a check for £250 to the 'entrepreneur' w the most original (and viable) bus proposal.

The award wil be called 'Business Idea of the Day'.

(The winner wl be ~~selected~~ chosen by all the expert present at the Seminar) — indent ½" at left & right

Save as EX2A and print one copy

Exercise 2b.

Please use justified margin, standardise layout and put 1st and last paras in double spacing. Use a line length of 55. Save as Ex 2B.

A GOOD PLACE TO WORK? ← spaced caps

An Exhibition for Office Workers

} centre & bold

The Information Tecnology revolution has changed the way we work and brought ~~with it~~ many benefits – both from the employers point of view and the employees angle. Altho' ~~Whilst~~ there are no serious occupational dangers such as you might find in an engineering workshop or a foundry, the office does have its own risks.

(underline paragraph headings and use lower case)

MANAGERS/SUPERVISORS Do you know what your responsibilities are under EC legislation?

ELECTRONIC OFFICE WORKERS/VDU OPERATORS Do you suffer from eye strain, aching shoulders, (back pain) headaches? What can you do to make your working day more comfortable? How can your ~~firm~~ employer help?

↕ 3 clear lines where this symbol is shown

VISIT THE GOOD PLACE TO WORK EXHIBITION

~~Learn how to~~ Help yourself to a better workpalce

} centre & bold

↕

It will be your job to assess every workstation ~~under~~ in your section/department. Its up to you to make sure EC recommendations are met.

The exhibition will offer:

- I____ Vidio (Inter-active)
- Slides
- Displays
- Quizzes, Questionnaires
- Proffessional Advice

The person to ask for on 'phone is: HAMISH HAMILTON

Exercise 2b.

continued

~~We can advise on~~ 3 areas ~~of concern~~: Learn about ↙ of interest ← CAPS, centre, no underline

Health (really)
Eye problems, muscular strain, repetitive strain injury, VDUs & pregnancy. Is it the (problems with) computers fault? What can be done to ~~alleviate~~ remove stress, worry and strain?

Ergonomics Workstations, systems, the workplace ~~as a whole~~ environment. Its ~~often easy~~ usually easy to change some aspects ~~eg~~ such as chairs, desks & lighting but its more difficult to change the way we think and work! [This is a very extensive topic – you'll be surprised whats involved.

SAFETY Electricity, Radiation, chemicals. Expediency can ~~mean~~ lead to inadequate and dangerous practises in /the use of electricity. There are many toxic chemicals in offices (but theres no risk provided due care is taken).

We'll give you the ~~evidence~~ facts about radiation from VDUs.

Exhibition ~~opens~~ starts at 1000 hrs Mon-Sat & closes at 6 pm Mon-Fri. (Early close Sat 1600 hrs.) Phone 071-124367 for exact location in yr town – ask for ____.

A G__ P__ T_ W__? ← spaced caps

CAPS → Appearing soon in a Car Park near you!

} centre & bold

In the Stage III Part 1 examination the 'header and footer' task usually extends to four pages. Refer to the glossary for instructions on setting headers, footers, and document pagination. You may be required to carry out any or all of the text editing techniques you have previously learned, but the instructions will be more complex and varied.

Read through the task before you attempt any reformatting procedures. Ensure you understand all the instructions and amendment signs, and that you don't miss any.

Footer command for automatic page numbering

If you need to show automatic page numbering with text, e.g. **PAGE NO 1**, **PAGE NO 2**, etc., you cannot use WordPerfect's standard method of page numbering command (**Shift** + **F8**, **2**, **7**).

Instead, you must set the page number via the footer command and **^B** (Press: **Ctrl key** + **B** to get **^B**):

Layout
Page

Press: **Shift** + **F8**
Select: **2** (Page) **4** (Footers)
1 (Footer A) **2** (Every page)
Type: **PAGE NO ^B** (Press **Ctrl** + **B** to get **^B**)
Press: **F7** twice to exit back to your document
Press: **Shift** + **F7**, **6** to **View Document** to make sure you have entered the '**PAGE NO #**' correctly.

Make sure you don't have WordPerfect's standard page numbering method turned on, or you will get two sets of numbers printed on the page.

Note: the hash sign (#) often symbolises automatic page numbering.

3.1 Practise operating the *footer command* to put on automatic page numbering. Enter the command: **PAGE NUMBER ^B** at bottom centre of footer screen.

Select *View Document* from the print menu to ensure you have entered it correctly. Clear your screen.

Handy tip

Deleting codes using search and replace

You can delete formatting codes throughout a document with one command by using the *search and replace* function.

Press: **Alt** + **F2**
Press: **Y** or **N** (to confirm each deletion or not as appropriate)
Press: **function keys normally used for the command you wish to delete** at **→ Srch**:
Press: **F2**
Press: **F2** at **Replace with**: (All the named codes are replaced with nothing, i.e. they are deleted.)

Quick move, copy and delete text

'Quick move' a block of text

```
Edit
Select
Sentence
Paragraph
Page
```

1 Position cursor anywhere within the text to be moved:

2 Press: **Ctrl + F4**

3 Press: **1** (if text to be moved is one sentence)
2 (if text to be moved is one paragraph)
3 (if text to be moved is one page)

Block of text is shaded on screen

4 Press: **1** (Move) (text disappears from screen)

5 Position cursor in new position for text

6 Press: ↵ (text appears in new position)

'Quick copy' a block of text

1, 2, 3 Repeat as for '*Quick move*':

4 Press: **2** (Copy)

5 Position cursor where a copy of text is to be placed

6 Press: ↵ (a copy of text appears in new position)

'Quick delete' a block of text

1, 2, 3 Repeat as for '*Quick move*':

4 Press: **3** (Delete) (text disappears from screen)

(Remember: if you delete a block of text in error, you can retrieve it by using the **F1** Cancel key.)

Handy tip

Quick 'name' search at List Files screen

If your list of files is very long you do not have to scroll down the list to find the file you want. You can do a name search:

Press: **N** (Name Search)
Type: **Filename** (name of file you require)
Press: ↵

Cursor will have jumped to file

3.2 **Exercise 3a.**

Retrieve the file **EX2A**. Refer to exercise headed *Exercise 3a* – you are asked to make a number of amendments to the document, including move, copy, delete functions, alter line spacing and margin justification, operate a search and replace command, and to enter a header and footer.

Because of the complexity of the task it would be easier to delete all existing formatting codes (line spacing, justification, page numbering, etc.) before you attempt to redesign the layout.

Press: **Alt** + **F3** or **F11** to bring up the reveal codes screen and work your way through the document, deleting any pre-set codes for line spacing, justification and page numbering.

Set the headers and document format as instructed on the exercise.

As it is a multi-page document you will need to put on page numbering, starting from page 2, as well as the specified text footer at the left-hand side of every page. To do this carry out steps (a) and (b) or steps (a) and (c) below:

a Using the footer command enter the text reference **REF: OU/SH** as Footer A at bottom left of every page.

b Using WordPerfect's standard method of page numbering, enter the page numbering position at bottom centre of page (remember to suppress page numbering for page 1). *The instructions for this task ensure that the page number does not overlap with the text reference at bottom left. You need to be aware of this when creating your own layouts.*

c As an alternative to step (b) you could enter automatic page number via Footer B using the **^B** command – notice that the page number is placed in a different position from Footer A. Also remember to suppress numbering on page 1.

Carry out all the amendments shown in Exercise 3a very carefully. Spellcheck and proofread your work thoroughly.

Save and *print* a copy of your document: use the filename **EX3A**.

Important

The RSA Stage III Part 1 examination requires candidates to proofread not only their own keyed-in work but *also the retrieved text*. There are often many spelling and grammatical errors in the text which has been keyed in prior to the exam by the tutor. Candidates should spellcheck and proofread the retrieved text very carefully indeed. This may be done before starting the task.

Handy tip

Searching and replacing codes

WordPerfect can search and replace codes as well as text. You could use this function to replace every bold code [**BOLD**] with an underline code [**UND**] throughout a document. You simply press the keys you would normally use to insert codes within the search and replace sequence.

Exercise 3a.

use a JUSTIFIED right margin throughout document
use SINGLE LINE SPACING except where specified differently

Exercise 3A

GOING IT ALONE SEMINAR — This line in spaced caps

Saturday (correct date inserted)

Opportunities Unlimited ~~are~~ is pleased to organise this Seminar for prospective business owners in the Boroughton area.

NB: Our offices are to be relocated in the West End Business Park, where our new, purpose-built accommodation is nearing completion. In the meantime, we are fortunate that we have been allowed to use the premises of the ~~Stratton~~ Vendôme Hotel, High Street, for our Seminar.

please move this paragraph to (A) and put in single line spacing

The seminar is the first of it's kind in the area & shd attract much publicity from the media. We are hoping to organise suitable press coverage, eg the local newspapers.

The required fee for the full day will be seventy-five pounds ~~including~~ including lunch.

The Seminar will be chaired by Neil Ross, Marketing Director of O——— U———.

indent these 2 paragraphs by 3" (75mm) at right margin to allow for a photograph

use the header: BUSINESS SEMINAR at top right of every page
use the footer: REF: OU/SH at bottom left of every page
and number the pages at bottom centre starting from page 2
KEEP THE PAGE BREAKS AS SHOWN

All this page to be in DOUBLE LINE SPACING please

Exercise 3a.

continued

(This line in CAPS)

The ~~Seminar will be held in the ground floor function suite and the~~ programme for the day has been organised as follows:

0900 HRS – INTRODUCTION

Neil Ross, Marketing Director of Opportunities Unlimited will outline the programme for the day. ~~and~~ He will introduce ~~the~~ the speakers and representatives from local industry, business and commerce, including:

1 Mr ~~David Wetherby~~ Ahmad Kahn – CHAIRMAN, Ridings & Holt Ltd

2 Mr Paul Knight – MANAGING DIRECTOR Vernons & Hoyle Ltd

3 Ms ~~Gladys~~ Gloria Fairway – MANAGING DIRECTOR Century ~~Enterprise~~ Systems

4 Mrs Vanessa Debarry – SOLICITOR Mayes, Drew & Smithies

(indent ½" (13mm) at left and right margins)

(align the dashes)

1000 HRS – START-UP SCHEMES

Presentations will be made by the High Street banks, the Small Business Advisory Service and the British Franchise Association.

Topics will include: ~~capital, loans, share issues, government schemes and development boards.~~

1100 HRS – COFFEE

(operator: please put all enumerated items in single line spacing but with one clear line between items)

i) Capital

ii) LOANS

5 ~~iii)~~ Share Issues

iv) goverment Schemes

3 ~~v)~~ Development Boards

vi) Organizational Skills

There will also be a short ~~talk~~ from Mr Alan Stevenson ~~from the~~ who will advice on help available thro' various Gov start-up schemes, e.g. financial assistance, administrative support etc.

Exercise 3a. *continued*

1115 HRS – WHAT MAKES AN ENTREPRENEUR?

With the aid of case histories, participants will be divided into groups + encouraged to discuss the viability of the respective businesses, types of business organisation, franchising, market research, and employment law. The ~~leader of each group~~ speakers for each topic will lead a 45-minute debate ~~advise~~ on Income Tax, VAT and National Insurance. The aim is to make the participants more aware of the pitfalls and pleasures ~~of~~ which come with self-employment.

The groups will then have an ~~opportunity~~ opp to put forward the main points from their discussions, including ~~all~~ any particular questions which remain unanswered.

(B)

leave 15 clear line spaces here

~~1245~~ 1.00 pm HRS – LUNCH IN 1ST FLOOR CARVERY

Exercise 3a. *continued*

1400 HRS – CONSULTATION SESSIONS

The 'experts' will make themselves available for individual consultation. Every participant can put forward his or her idea and, in return, receive valuable assistance along with constructive criticism.

There will be a short 10-minute interval half way through this session.

1600 HRS – PLENARY SESSION/PRIZE PRESENTATION

Neil Ross, Marketing Director, will present an award – 'Business Idea of the Day' – together with a cheque for ~~£250~~ £175.00 to the 'entrepreneur' with the most original (and viable) business proposal.

(The winner will be chosen by ~~all~~ the panel of experts present at the Seminar.)

Leave at least 10 clear line spaces here

This sentence in CAPS and DOUBLE LINE SPACING – retain indented style

USE A LINE LENGTH OF 46 FOR THIS PARAGRAPH AND DOUBLE LINE SPACING. COPY IT TO (B) – USE THE SAME SETTINGS

(A)

Replace the name Neil Ross with the name Adam Flynn throughout the document

Exercise 3b.

Clear your screen. Retrieve the file **EX2B**. Refer to the exercise headed *Exercise 3b* and follow all the instructions carefully. *Save* and *print* a copy of your document: use the filename **EX3B**.

Change to a RAGGED right margin throughout
Use SINGLE LINE SPACING unless it is specified otherwise

Exercise 3b

A G O O D P L A C E T O W O R K ?

An Exhibition for Office Workers

copy this line to ✱

The Information Technology revolution has changed ~~the way we work~~ our working lives and brought ~~many~~ numerous benefits - both from the employer's point of view and the employees' angle. Although there are no serious occupational dangers (such as you might find in an engineering workshop or a foundry), ~~the~~ office ~~does have its own risks.~~ ~~environment~~ environment

their are still risks involved for those who work in an

single line spacing

Managers/Supervisors Do you know exactly what your responsibilities are under EC legislation?

It ~~will be~~ is your job to assess the safe working order of every workstation in your section/department. It's up to you to make sure EC recommendations are met.

you shd ask ~~yourself~~ the following questions:

Electronic Office Workers/VDU Operators ~~Do~~ If you suffer from eye strain, aching shoulders, back pain, headaches? // 1) What can you do to make your working day more comfortable? // 2) How can your employer help?

3) Are you taking suff breaks away from the VDU screen

4) Is the office furniture adequate, eg chair set to correct height and is a backrest?

5) ~~Is~~ Is the air-conditioning affective?

6) Have you had your eyesight checked by an an optician since you started working on a V.D.U?

New gov laws are now in effect wh regulate the no of hrs an operator may sit at a VDU without a brake.

OPERATOR: keep this section together as Page 1

indent enumerated items 12 spaces from left margin and use single line spacing with one clear line space between items - use the same style for any other enumerated items in the document

Exercise 3b. *continued*

VISIT THE GOOD PLACE TO WORK EXHIBITION

Help yourself to a better workplace

(move this section so it becomes page 3 – leave rest of page blank)

(this line in CAPS)

The exhibition will offer:

a) Inter-active Video
b) Slides
c) Displays from leading mfrs
d) Professional Advice from the many experts who will be on hand to deal w yr individual problems
e) Quizzes, Questionnaires

There will also be an Information Stand offering advice on EC legislation.

THERE WILL BE CONTINUOUS LECTURES ~~LEARN~~ ABOUT 3 AREAS OF INTEREST:

Health Eye problems, muscular strain, repetitive strain injury, VDUs and pregnancy. ~~Is it~~ Are all health problems really the computer's fault? What can be done to alleviate stress, strain and worry?

Ergonomics Workstations, systems, the workplace environment. It's usually easy to change some aspects such as chairs, desks, and lighting but it's more difficult to change the way we think and work!

This is a very extensive topic – you'll be surprised what's involved. (you'll, what's – in full)

OPERATOR:

- use the header EXHIBITION at top right
- use the footer OFFICE WORKERS at bottom right
- number the pages at bottom left starting on page 2
- follow the instructions given for page breaks

Exercise 3b. *continued*

keep this paragraph on the "..... 3 AREAS OF INTEREST" page

Safety Electricity, radiation, chemicals. Expediency can lead to inadequate and dangerous practices in the use of electricity. There are many toxic chemicals in offices (but there's no risk provided due care is taken). We'll give you the facts about radiation from VDUs.

– 95% of accidents are caused through negligence

Exhibition opens at ~~1000~~ 9.30 am hrs Monday – Saturday and closes at

1800 hrs Monday – Friday. (Early close Saturday 1600 hrs.)

Phone 071-1243̶6̶7 for exact location in your ~~town~~ area – ask for

Hamish Hamilton.

Admission fee: £1.00 Adults
£0.50p Children (accompanied)
fifty pence OAPs

Parties of 10 or more qualify for a ten per cent discount.

leave 7 clear lines here

A GOOD PLACE TO WORK?
APPEARING SOON ~~IN A CAR PARK~~ NEAR YOU!
centre

OPENING TIMES

Insert as a heading where shown and start a new page (p4). Use DOUBLE LINE SPACING for all of page 4

please set the line length for this section only to 46

OPERATOR: replace the abbreviation EC with European Community throughout the document

Printing out arrangements in the RSA Stage III Part 1 examination

You are given 10 sheets of A4 paper and two pre-printed 'Praxiteles' letterheads for this examination. (*Put your letterheads on one side to ensure they are not used for draft printing.*)

This is sufficient to be able to print out the following:

One *final* copy of the two-page document
One *final* copy of the four-page document
One *final* copy of the letter on letterhead

You will then have four sheets of plain paper with which to print draft copies for checking during the examination. The letter may take one or two sheets so if you print a draft copy, you will then have to decide to use the remaining two or three sheets in one of the following ways:

1 Print a draft copy of the two-page document

2 Print a draft copy of *one page* of the two-page document *and* a draft copy of *one page* of the four-page document (*to check headers etc.*)

3 Print a draft copy of *two pages* of the *four-page* document

You should make sure that you have previously practised printing on RSA's 'Praxiteles' letterheads using the same equipment that will be available for your examination.

The printing of the final copies of the tasks in this examination is done outside the examination time of one-and-a-quarter hours *by the candidate.*

No amendments may be made to the text after that time has expired, and in WordPerfect the printing is done from the List Files screen. (*There is no need to retrieve the document to print.*)

You are allowed to insert special characters, such as accents, on to the final copies after the examination time. Use a black pen for this.

The invigilator at your examination centre will explain the procedures to be followed for printing in that centre.

Handy tip

Shift + F3 switch

If your screen suddenly goes blank and you notice that **Doc 2** is showing on the status line, you may have pressed **Shift** + **F3** by mistake. To get back to your work, press **Shift** + **F3** again.

Exercise Con1a.

CON 1A – Key in this letter to Mrs U Adamson, Careers Teacher, Queen Anne's High School, Wellington Gr, BURNDALE, BE2 5AB. Use a ragged right margin and mark URGENT.

Save & print one copy. Filename: CON 1A

Dear Mrs A___

VISITORS DAY ← lower case, initial caps & underscore

I am writing to tell you about next weeks Visitors Day at our College. Altho' it is rather short notice, I hope you wl be able to attend, along w members of yr staff and pupils. ≠ I must apologise for the letters lateness; ~~this~~ is due to the fact that we have been ✓ waiting for the ~~printing~~ arrival of our brochure and application forms to be completed. (copies enclosed)

We bel ~~it~~ the V___ D___ is an excellant opp for school pupils to get the info they require and to exp a day in the working life of the College. Pupils can view the accom & rec advice & help in selecting a course to suit them. The College Admissions Dept wl be available to make sep appts for those ~~students~~ pupils who wishes to make a def commitment to a f/t course.

The college wl be open ~~from~~ between the hrs of 9am & 1900 hrs on Thurs (next Thurs date) & a buffet lunch is wl be served in the ___________ for a limited number of careers ~~officers~~ teachers. I am sending a copy of this letter to the Head of your 6th Form. Please return the enclosed form if you wish to join us for lunch – or telephone my sec on ext 3164 asap. ← Indent 1st para by ½" at left

Lunch wl be in the Training Restaurant

Yrs scly

M/J CRABTREE

Marketing Officer, B___ Tertiary College

Exercise Con1b.

Please key in, using a ragged right margin. Save as CON1B and print one copy. Standardise layout of headings to lowercase with underscore.

BURNDALE TERTIARY COLLEGE
Shaftesbury Road
BURNDALE BE1 3WB
} centre

BUSINESS ADMINISTRATION – centre & spaced caps

double spacing

Full-time Courses [Bus Admin courses are related to National Vocational Qualifications (NVQs). Students ~~study~~ follow a ~~course~~ programme based on there previous exp & qualifications and designed to meet ~~their~~ each individuals needs. All courses run for 1 year but may be extended to two yrs for those who wish to improve their qualifications and job prospects. (at levels 2, 3 & 4)

THE BUS ADMIN PROGRAMME

The ~~basic~~ core subjects are:

Typewriting
Word Processing
Computer Applications

The timetable is organized in such a way that students can then ~~add~~ choose additional ~~options~~ choices from the the following list:

Shorthand	Book-keeping
Audio-typewriting	European Studies
Desk Top Publishing	French for Business*
German for Business*	Statistics for Business*

* A GCSE grade A-C in the relevant language is necessary in order to begin studying languages for business, and (Mathematics) for Statistics for business.

Our courses provide an excellent starting point for a career in the bus world. The skills learned can be transferred to many different jobs at different levels – from office junior to managing director.

The Admissions Officer is Jenny McEwan

Exercise Con1b. *continued*

Practical Experience

The majority of the work are practical in nature & students work at their own pace. Work placements are a valuble part of all are courses. Students work in local businesses for three weeks - one week ~~each~~ per term in a 3-term coarse.

HOW TO APPLY

An application form may be ~~filled in~~ completed at any time - not just during the Spring and Summer terms. It can be a def advantage to apply early as the courses are popular. Forms shd be recd by the Admissions Officer, ____ ____, by the end of June so that preliminary interviews can be organised. However, late applications are very welcome. Its never too late!

COMMENCEMENT OF COURSES The courses wl begin on Mon 9 Sept at 9 am. ~~Attendance~~ Lessons (✓) is from 0900 hrs to 5 pm each day except Wednesday when the afternoon are left free for leisure/creative pursuits.

COME TO ~~VISIT~~ OUR ~~OPEN~~ VISITORS DAY
Thurs (insert date)
0900 – 1900 hrs
] centre

Exercise Con1c.

Retrieve the file **EXCON1B**. Follow all the instructions shown. Use *double line spacing* unless it is specified otherwise. *Save* and *print* a copy of your work – use the filename *EXCON1C*

BURNDALE TERTIARY COLLEGE
Shaftesbury Road
BURNDALE BE1 3WB
} single line spacing

COURSES IN ^ B U S I N E S S   A D M I N I S T R A T I O N ← closed caps + underline

Full time Courses

Business Administration courses are ~~related to~~ (centred around) National Vocational Qualifications (NVQs) at levels ~~II~~, ~~III~~ and ~~IV~~ (2, 3 and 4). Students follow a ^ 'modular' programme ^ (the structure of which is) based on their previous experience and qualifications. ~~and designed to meet each individual's needs~~. All courses run for 1 year ^ from Sep - June but may be extended to 2 years for those who wish to improve their job prospects ^ ~~and~~ & advanced qualifications.

Our courses provide an excellent ~~starting point~~ (basis) for a career in the business world (transpose: world of business). The skills learned can be transferred to many different jobs at different levels - from Office Junior to Managing Director.

(A)

CHANGE ALL SHOULDER HEADINGS TO CAPS AND REMOVE UNDERLINE

OPERATOR:
use the header (at top left of every page): BA/COURSES

use a footer (at bottom centre of every page) to number the pages in the format of: PAGE No1, PAGE No2 ..... starting on page 2

Keep the page breaks as indicated in the draft

Exercise Con1c. *continued*

The Business Administration Programme

The core subjects are:

inset 1" from left margin

Typewriting
Word Processing
Computer Applications

Office Administration

The timetable is organized in such a way that students can then choose additional options from the following list:

inset 1" from left margin

Shorthand	Book-keeping
Audio-typewriting	European Studies
German for Business*	French for Business*
Desk Top Publishing	Statistics for Business*

* A GCSE grade A-C in ~~the relevant language~~ German or French is necessary in order to begin studying the languages for business and in mathematics for "Statistics for Business".

shorten line length of this paragraph to 50

Practical Experience

The majority of the ~~work~~ training is practical in nature and students work at their own pace. Work ~~placements are~~ exp is a valuable part of all our courses. Students carry out "real work" in local businesses for 3 weeks - 1 week per term in a 3-term course.

In the past, we have (wherever poss) organized a different work placement for each of the three weeks.

The College is proud of it's tecnology, e.g. 3 rooms of new up-to-date computers, two colour laser printers and a range of ~~[illegible]~~ industry-standard softwear packages.

Use SINGLE LINE SPACING for inset sections and for the paragraph with line length shortened to 50

Exercise Con1c. *continued*

(B)

please change the word organized to organised throughout the document

How to Apply

Application forms for f/t courses

An application form may be completed at any time ~~– not just during the Spring and Summer terms~~. It can be a definite advantage to apply early as the courses are popular. ~~Forms~~ should be received by the Admissions Officer, Jenny McEwan, by the end of June so that preliminary interviews can be organized. However, late applications are very welcome. It's never too late!

Commencement of Courses

~~The~~ All f/t courses ~~will begin~~ commence on Monday 9 September at 9.00 am. ~~Attendance is from 9.00 am to 5.00 pm each day except Wednesday when the afternoon is left free for leisure/creative pursuits.~~ // Enrolment dates for p/t courses are available from the College Reception & are also published 2 weeks prior to commencement in the local press.

move this section to (B)

LEAVE 11 CLEAR LINES HERE

COME TO OUR VISITORS DAY

Thursday (correct date inserted)

9.00 am – 7.00 pm

copy to (A)

PART TIME COURSES

We ~~offer~~ a ~~full~~ wide range of part time courses either in single subjects (e.g. typewriting, word processing, shorthand) and also in B______ A______ NVQ Levels 3 and 2. Some examples of this are listed below:

LEAVE REST OF PAGE BLANK FOR A LIST TO BE PHOTOCOPIED ONTO PAGE LATER

insert this section as Page 3

General hints

You will already know how to complete a simple form with given information. In this unit you are going to carry out the actual design of the form using given headings/items.

1. Include all given headings/items and arrange these in a logical manner – use your initiative for the layout.
2. Allow suitable space after each heading/item displayed so that the relevant information can be inserted later.
3. Decide whether the information that is to be inserted later will be carried out by hand, on a typewriter or on a word processor. This will determine the method of layout, i.e. should the allocated space take the form of dotted lines or enter points?
4. Follow instructions for allocating space of specified size (*vertically and horizontally*) for illustrations/photographs etc.
5. Give prominence to (*highlight*) specified headings/items in the form.
6. Make good use of the paper size (i.e. don't squash everything together!) The end result should look clear and presentable.

IMPORTANT

This unit contains instruction on advanced form-design techniques to produce special effects such as line-drawing, shaded boxes etc. However, these features are *not essential* requirements of the Stage III examination and have only been included as sample preparation for the workplace and/or personal interest.

It would be unwise for examination candidates to spend too much time on producing unnecessary special effects for the form-design tasks at the expense of successfully completing the table and mail merge tasks.

For the examination, therefore, complete the form design task using the simplest and quickest methods; only use special effects *after* you have completed all the other examination tasks.

Methods of space allocation

Dotted lines

When leaving rows of dotted lines remember to leave one space before the first dot. It is usually good practice to end all the dotted lines at the same position. You should also use double line spacing (or more) to allow sufficient room for the information to be inserted.

Example: Surname ....

First Name ....

Age .... Date of Birth ....

Enter points

Choose a suitable symbol for the enter points which does not normally appear in the text, e.g. * or $. This will enable the operator who will complete the form later (by using the search facility to locate the enter points and replace them with the appropriate information) to do so with greater ease.

Example: Surname $

First Name $

Age $ Date of Birth $

Remember: when allocating vertical space six clear lines = 1 in.

Methods of display

Change the font size and appearance

As well as using **bold**, <u>underline</u> or S P A C E D C A P S to highlight items, you may also choose to select the following.

```
Font
Appearance
Italics
```

Italics

Press: **Ctrl** + **F8**
Select: **2** (Appearance)
Select: **4** (Italic)
Key in text

Larger fonts

```
Font
Large
or Very large
or Extra large
```

Press: **Ctrl** + **F8**
Select: **1** (Size)
Select: **5** (Large) or **6** (Very Large) or **7** (Extra Large)
Key in text

To return to normal text

```
Font
Normal
```

Press: **Ctrl** + **F8**
Select: **3** (Normal)
Key in text

You may like to try out some of the other options listed under the **Ctrl** + **F8** key, e.g. double underline, shadow, etc.

To change size or appearance of text already keyed in:

```
Edit
Block
```

Block the text to be altered with **F12** or **Alt** + **F4**
Continue with **Ctrl** + **F8** to select changes required

Important: the type of printer you are using will determine which methods of display can be supported, as some printers are not capable of utilising all of WordPerfect's features. Check with your tutor or printer manual and/or print a draft test copy to try out the different effects.

4.1 **Exercise 4a.**

Clear your screen. Key in your name and the task number on line 1. Design and prepare the membership form below leaving adequate amounts of space for insertions at *.

Change the word '*Disco*' to '*Dance*' wherever it occurs in this task. *Save* and *print* a copy of your work – use the file name **EX4A**.

JUNIOR MEMBERSHIP FORM ← spaced caps + centre

Jo-Jo Junior Disco Team

Surname *

First Name *

Age *

Date of Birth *

Sex *

also include the headings, Address, Tel No and Membership No

leave space here 2" across by 1½" down (51mm × 38mm) for a photograph

Attending: JAZZ – Monday
MODERN DISCO – Wednesday
BALLET – Friday
CREATIVE DISCO – Sat
(please tick sessions to be attended)

Fee Paid *

Date of Joining *

give prominence to the Attending: section

Handy tip

Version 5.1

To superimpose a text heading on a grey bar:

Create a single cell-table	Type text into cell
Alt + **F7**	Press: **Alt** + **F7** (Table Edit)
2 (Tables)	**3** (Lines)
1 (Create)	**8** (Shade)
No. of Columns 1 ↵	**1** (On)
No. of Rows 1 ↵	**3** (Lines)
F7 (Exit Table Edit)	**7** (All)
	1 (None)

```
Layout
Tables
Create
```

Ruled lines – by line draw (Ctrl + F3)

Not all printers support line draw – check with your tutor and/or printer manual and print out a test copy if you are still not sure. It is a useful facility for drawing lines and boxes and can be used to enhance the appearance of the form.

However, it can produce some unpredictable results if care is not taken, particularly when inserting the vertical lines of the table when the characters can tend to 'jump' out of position. After exiting line draw, if you move the cursor through the columns, the characters will usually 'jump' back into place!

```
Layout
Line
Line Height
```

Another problem with using line draw for vertical lines is that on printing out most printers will leave small gaps between the lines unless you increase the line height via the format menu (**Shift + F8**, **1**: **Line**, **4**: **Line Height**).

Where time is of the essence in an examination situation, the authors feel there are drawbacks in your spending a lot of time getting it right! No doubt many students will love the line draw facility and prove us wrong!

The line draw facility can be useful for inserting horizontal lines with any vertical lines being inserted after printing by hand. To operate line draw:

```
Tools
Line Draw
```

Press: **Ctrl + F3**
Select: **2** (Line Draw)
Select: **1**, **2**, or **3** or .....
Select: **4** (Change) to view the different options

The line will begin wherever the cursor is positioned on screen. Press the arrow keys to draw the line in the required direction.

Select: **6** (Move) to stop line draw until you re-position the cursor – you will then need to re-select the line to commence drawing again
Select: **5** (Erase) to rub out any incorrect line using the arrow keys

To enter text into a drawn box, you must be in *typeover* mode.

To draw around existing text, you must indent the text several spaces or it will be erased by the lines going over it.

Ruled lines – by graphics line

This feature is useful but needs plenty of practice for it to be mastered. Refer to your manufacturer's manual for instructions if you wish to try this feature

4.2 Exercise 4b.

Clear your screen. Key in your name and the task number on line 1. Design and prepare a telephone message form. Save and print a copy of your work – use the filename **EX4B**.

Include the following headings where appropriate and leave suitable space for each item:

MESSAGE FOR, DATE, TIME, CALLER'S NAME, CALLER'S COMPANY, CALLER'S TEL NO

TELEPHONE MESSAGE ← centre + underline

ACTION: URGENT/NON URGENT
RING BACK
WILL CALL AGAIN LATER

give prominence to the ACTION section

leave a space 2" across by 1" down (51mm x 25mm) for companyname and stamp

MESSAGE ______

______

______

______

______

Received by ______ Date ______

In the RSA Stage III examination the table contains a number of additional features to those at Stage II.

In addition to normal editing and tabulation procedures you will also be required to:

- include at least two footnotes in the form of superscripted numbers
- divide the columns of the table by a ruled line horizontally or vertically as specified
- enter horizontal and/or vertical column headings
- modify the layout as instructed
- rule the table (either by hand and/or on machine)

You should refresh your memory on the instructions for reducing the pitch size, altering margin settings, wrapping text on to next column, explanation of footnotes and methods of rearranging the table items.

Note: a 'superscripted' character is printed slightly above the standard line, e.g. 8.5^2

Footnotes with superscripted number – manual method

You can enter the superscripted footnote as follows: position the cursor immediately after the word/character requiring a footnote, then proceed as follows.

Change the font to superscript

```
Font
Superscript
```

Press: **Ctrl** + **F8**
Select: **1** (Size) **1** (Suprscpt)

Key in the footnote number – remember, there is *no space before* a footnote number in the body of the text.

Revert to normal text

```
Font
Normal
```

Press: **Ctrl** + **F8**
Select: **3** (Normal)

Note: the footnote number at the bottom of the page/document, with the explanatory text next to it, does *not* need to be in superscript.

Handy tip

To repeat a character a specified number of times, use the **Esc** key to repeat value. The repetition number default is usually set to 5, but it can be changed temporarily or permanently. For example:

To draw a line of 15 equal signs
Press: **Esc 15 =**

To move up 12 lines:
Press: **Esc 12 ↑**

Footnotes – WordPerfect's command method

Footnote command

```
Layout
Footnote
Create
```

WordPerfect has a clever feature that makes creating footnotes much easier.

Position cursor immediately next to the text to have a footnote.

Press: **Ctrl** + **F7**
Select: **1** (Footnote) **1** (Create)

The footnote screen appears with a message to press *exit* when done at bottom left.

The footnote number (automatically provided for you by WordPerfect) is *to the left of the cursor.*

Press: **the space bar** (to leave a space between the number and explanatory text)
Type: **the explanatory text** for the footnote
Press: **F7** to exit the footnote screen

WordPerfect automatically places the superscripted footnote number in the body of the text, and the explanatory footnote at the bottom of the page/document. As with headers and footers, however, you cannot see the explanatory footnote on your screen. You can view it if you press **Shift** + **F7** and choose the *View Document* option, and the codes can be seen in the reveal codes screen.

Edit the footnote

```
Layout
Footnote
Edit
```

Press: **Ctrl** + **F7**
Select: **1** (Footnote) **2** (Edit)

Make the necessary changes – use normal editing methods
Press: **F7** (Exit)

Delete the footnote

Position cursor on footnote number and press the delete key.

Answer the screen prompt: **Delete [Footnote: 1]? (Y/N) No** with **Y**

Move the footnote

```
Block footnote
Edit
Move
Move cursor
Paste
```

Delete the footnote as above. Move cursor to new position: press **F1** (the Restore key) and select **1** (Restore).

Footnote display options

This feature allows you to alter several footnote display features. By selecting the appropriate option, you can alter such features as:

- spacing within or between footnotes
- numbering mode, e.g. take off the superscript code for the explanatory footnote which goes at the bottom of the page
- length of separating line, or even remove it altogether

To change the footnote display

```
Layout
Footnote
Options
```

Press: **Ctrl** + **F7**
Select: **1** (Footnote)
Select: **4** (Options) (the Footnote Options screen appears)

a *To alter the numbering style*

(so that the explanatory footnote number at bottom of page/document is *not superscripted* and also to remove the indent):
Select: **4** – *style for number in note*
Replace with: **[SUPERSCPT][Note num][superscpt]** appears at bottom of screen
Position cursor on first blank space after: **Replace with**: Delete *all* the blank spaces immediately before the **[SUPERSCPT]** code
Position cursor on the first superscript code: **[SUPERSCPT]**
Delete the code and press **return**
Press: **F7** to return to your document

b *To remove the 2 in line separating text and footnotes*

Select: **7** – *Line separating text and footnotes* (The default line length is set at 2 in)
Select: **1** – *No Line*

c *To alter position of footnotes at bottom of page*

Select: **9** – *Footnotes at bottom of page* (The default is usually set to 'Yes')
Type: **N**(o) (This will alter the position of the explanatory footnotes to just beneath the exercise)

Handy tip

Subscripted characters

If your printer will support this, you can format characters to appear slightly below the 'typing line', e.g. CO_2, H_2O.

Press: **Ctrl** + **F8**
Press: **1** (Size)
Press: **2** (Subscript)
Type: **character to be subscripted**
Press: **→** (to exit subscript mode)

5.1 **Exercise 5a.**

Clear your screen. Key in your name and the task number on line 1. Before going on to the table let's practise inserting footnotes using WordPerfect's footnote facility. Key in the following passage:

```
The Huns were a nomad people once scattered widely in
Asia in the steppe country, north of the Caspian Sea.
They were short in stature with black hair, yellow skins,
broad noses and deep-set eyes. They settled, in the 5th
century, north of the Danube in the lands which are now
Austria and Hungary, and dominated the peoples under
their leader, Attila for some time.
```

5.2 Position the cursor immediately after the 's' of 'Huns' in the first line of the passage above.

Layout Footnote Create

Press: **Ctrl** + **F7**
Select: **1** (Footnote) **1** (Create)
Press: **F4** (use indent key instead of space bar to align the paragraph)
Type: **The word 'Hun' has no reference to the German descent, but denotes ferocity and destructiveness.**
Press: **F7** to exit the footnote screen

5.3 Position the cursor immediately after the 'y' of 'Hungary'

Press: **Ctrl** + **F7**
Select: **1** (Footnote) **1** (Create)
Press: **F4**
Type: **In spite of their name, the Hungarians have no connection with the Huns.**
Press: **F7** to exit the footnote screen

5.4

Press: **Shift** + **F7** and select the *View Document* option to view your work – choose option **3** to view the full page so that you can see the explanatory footnotes placed at the bottom of the page. It should look as below:

```
The Huns[1] were a nomad people once scattered widely in
Asia in the steppe country, north of the Caspian Sea.
They were short in stature with black hair, yellow skins,
broad noses and deep-set eyes. They settled, in the 5th
century, north of the Danube in the lands which are now
Austria and Hungary[2], and dominated the peoples under
their leader, Attila for some time.




--------------------

1     The word 'Hun' has no reference to the German
      descent, but denotes ferocity and destructiveness.

2     In spite of their name, the Hungarians have no
      connection with the Huns.
```

5.5

You are now going to change some of the options for the footnote display. Position the cursor at start of the passage on screen. Refer to the instructions headed '*footnote display options*' and follow steps (a), (b) and (c) in order to:

a Alter the numbering style of the footnote number in the explanatory text at the bottom of the page so it does not appear superscripted, and also remove the preceding indent;

b remove the 2 in line separating text and footnotes;

c alter the position of the explanatory footnotes so they appear just below the exercise instead of at the bottom of the page.

5.6

Press: **Shift** + **F7** and select the *View Document* option again to view your amendments. It should now look as below:

The Huns[1] were a nomad people once scattered widely in Asia in the steppe country, north of the Caspian Sea. They were short in stature with black hair, yellow skins, broad noses and deep-set eyes. They settled, in the 5th century, north of the Danube in the lands which are now Austria and Hungary[2], and dominated the peoples under their leader, Attila for some time.

1 **The word 'Hun' has no reference to the German descent, but denotes ferocity and destructiveness.**

2 **In spite of their name, the Hungarians have no connection with the Huns.**

Vertical column headings

Vertical column headings are relatively simple to enter using a word processor. The heading takes up one character per line and is read downwards instead of across. The number of characters in the heading will determine the length of the vertical column heading area.

Example:

ITEM Description	P A G E
Dungarees	4
Jumpers	6
Skirts	2

Ruled lines – by underscore/hand

There are several ways of ruling lines on to the table – they can even be put on by hand in black pen!

If you have WordPerfect Version 5.1 you may use the *table facility* – see separate instructions.

If you have WordPerfect Version 5.0, the authors believe that the simplest method is to enter a line of underscores for the horizontal lines and rule in the vertical lines after printing by hand using a fine clean, black pen and a 30 cm ruler with a smooth edge.

Extreme care should be taken to ensure that the lines are drawn neatly and accurately – no smudges, gaps where lines should join, or missed lines! Take care, also, not to extend the line beyond its correct position, particularly where the lines meet at a corner. In the examination every incorrect line is penalised!

Horizontal lines using underscore

```
Edit
Block
(shadeline)
Edit
Delete
(Move cursor)
Undelete
```

A quick method of repeating a horizontal line is to use the **underscore** and **F1** Cancel key:

Enter the first horizontal line using the underscore.
Delete the line in the normal way (position cursor at beginning of line and Press: **Ctrl + End**)
Press: **F1** (Cancel key) and select **1** (Restore) (to restore the deleted line immediately)
Reposition the cursor where you want another horizontal line to appear:
Press: **F1:** *Cancel* and choose **1:** *Restore*
Repeat for each horizontal line required.

WordPerfect does have line-drawing facilities as described in Unit 4, but it is recommended that the program manual should be consulted for in-depth instruction; neither line draw nor graphics line is entirely suitable to meet the complexities of the table task.

Table facility – Version 5.1

```
Layout
Subscript
```

The table feature of Version 5.1 makes data entry into multiple columns of varying width a relatively simple procedure. It certainly simplifies the entry of any tabular data for tables, invoices, etc.

The table consists of rows and columns divided into cells like a spreadsheet.

You can set up the table format before entering your text (i.e. specify number of columns and rows, cell-width, etc.) – it is also easy to edit the table if you need to make any changes later on. As with any other advanced feature, you will need to practise before you are confident and can produce a table quickly, but your practice will be worth the effort.

Table facility

```
Layout
Tables
Create
```

Press: **Alt** + **F7** **2** (Tables) **1** (Create)
Key in: **no of columns required** ↵
Key in: **no of rows required** ↵

The *Table Edit* screen appears. The cell in which the cursor is positioned is shaded (red).

To move between the cells:
Press: **Alt** + **one of the arrow keys** (in the appropriate direction)
or
Press: **Tab** key (to move right)
Shift + **Tab** key (to move left)

To increase width of a cell:
Press: **Ctrl** + →

To decrease width of a cell:
Press: **Ctrl** + ←

To insert a row/column:
Press: **Ins** key
Select: **Rows or Columns**
Enter: **Number of Rows/Columns to Insert** ↵

To delete a row/column:
Press: **Del** key
Select: **Row or Column**
Enter: **Number of Rows/Columns to Delete**

To move/copy text in a cell:
Use WordPerfect's standard block and move/copy functions to move or copy any data inside a cell to another part of the table.

To delete text in a cell:
Position cursor immediately after text to be deleted in the cell where text is to be deleted and press ← **Del** (backspace delete key)

Table Menus

The menu at the foot of the Table Edit screen (**Alt** + **F7**) offers the following functions:

1 Size: to re-size the table completely and re-enter the number of rows and columns required.

2 Format: **a** to determine type of data to be entered into a cell as **1: Numeric** or **2: Text**

b to determine attributes of a cell or column such as *Appearance*, *Size*, *Justification*, etc. You can also specify the *number of decimal places* in a column through the **2: Column, 4: Number digits** option.

3 Lines: to change the type of line display, e.g. double line, single line, thick line, dotted line or even no lines. You can alter the lines individually (i.e. top, left, inside, etc.) or choose the **all** option to make all the lines of the table the same.

There is also a **shade** option that you can turn on or off to shade (darken) any of the cells. Although shading is not visible on screen, you can choose the View Document option from the Print Menu to see how it will look. This feature is often used for cells that contain headings to make them stand out.

4 Header: to define a header row (or rows) to be repeated at top of every page. (You will not need this option for RSA Stage III.)

5 Maths: to enter formulae and perform calculations. (You will not need this option for RSA Stage III.)

6 Options: to change layout such as spacing between text and lines, position of table, percentage of grey shading, etc. (You will not need this option for RSA Stage III.)

7 Join: To block the cells you wish to join, press: **Alt** + **F4** or **F12** then select this option to merge cells together. This is useful for multi-line and/or multi-column headings.

8 Split: to split one cell into two (or more) select: **Split Rows/Columns**

Enter: **Number of Rows/Columns in which cell is to be split.**

WordPerfect will adjust the height of all cells in that row/column to allow for the new cells. (You can split several cells at the same time by blocking them first with **F12** or **Alt** + **F4**.)

The *status line* at bottom right of screen tells you which cell the cursor is in.

5.7 Exercise 5b.

Clear your screen. Key in your name and the task number on line 1. Set left and right margins at ½ in to enter the table shown on page 46.

If you are using Version 5.1 and wish to use the table facility follow the instructions headed: *Setting up the table – Version 5.1.*

If you are using Version 5.0, or do not wish to use the table facility, follow the instructions headed: *Setting up the table – Version 5.0.*

Setting up the table – Version 5.0

Work from the layout for the table, Exercise 5b.

When entering tab settings, note that you will also need to set a tab for the first column (CAT REF NO) at **12** to allow for the vertical line to be placed at the left margin at **10**. Therefore, set tabs for the column headings at: **12**, **18**, **37**, **50**, **58**, **66**.

After entering the column headings delete the tab settings at **50** and **58** and replace with **decimal** tab settings at *52* and *60*.

Enter the horizontal and vertical lines using the most appropriate method available to you – it is largely up to the individual to try these out and adopt the method he/she can comfortably complete within the time limit of the Stage III examination, and within the scope of the program version and printer being used. Refer to page 43 Ruled Lines – by underscore/hand.

Setting up the table – Version 5.1

```
Layout
Tables
Create
```

1 Press: **Alt** + **F7** **2** (Tables) **1** (Create)
Enter: **6 columns and 6 rows** (you need 4 rows for each of the items plus 2 rows for the multi-line heading)

2 Position cursor in cell **A1**
Press: **Ctrl** + ← *five times* (to decrease cell width for CAT REF NO column)

3 Position cursor in cell **B1**
Press: **Ctrl** + → *seven times* (to increase cell width for STOCK DESCRIPTION column)

4 Position cursor in cell **C1**
Press: **Ctrl** + → *three times* (to increase cell width for SIZE column)

5 Position cursor in cell **F1** (column with vertical heading, PAGE)
Decrease the cell width until it is only one character wide

6 Leave the width of cells **D1** and **E1** as they are – you will edit these later. Don't worry if you haven't quite got the widths of the cells absolutely correct at this stage. You can go in and out of *Table Edit* increasing/decreasing cell width whenever necessary.

7 Press: **F7** to exit the Table Edit screen.
Your table should now look as below:

8 Enter the table text: position the cursor in cell **A1** and enter the heading CAT REF NO, pressing the return key after each word.
Press **Tab** key to move to cell **B1** and enter next heading, STOCK DESCRIPTION.

9 Continue entering the headings into the cells, using the **Tab** key or **Alt** + **arrow** keys to move between the cells. Note that the cells will 'expand' vertically to accommodate longer portions of text as you enter it, allowing the text to 'wrap' on to another line, e.g. the vertical column heading PAGE.

10 Enter the rest of the table text and data. Press **Alt** + **F7** to return to Table Edit mode.

11 Position the cursor in any cells which you think should be decreased or increased in width (e.g. *D2, E2*) and alter as appropriate. (If you make a column too narrow, text will be 'wrapped round' on to the next line in the same column.)

You should enter the multi-column headings -10 and 10+ in their appropriate positions on the second row. Don't worry at this stage about the rest of the blank cells on row 2 – you will join them together shortly.

12 You can enter the table footnotes using any of the methods described previously. Your table should now look as below:

CAT REF NO	STOCK DESCRIPTION	SIZE	COST[1]		P A G E
			-10	10+	
QW3	Vax Audio Case	18" x 13"	9.99	7.99	2
QW5	Eva Audio Case[2]	12" x 7"	7.99	6.99	4
QW7	Gem Audio Case	18" x 13"	9.99	8.99	1
QW8	Seva Audio Case	18" x 15"	6.99	5.99	3

1 Bulk orders of 50+ qualify for a further discount.

2 Available in black, red or green.

13 Press: **F7** to exit Table Edit. Select the *View Document* option from the *Print Menu* to see how the table will look.
Press: **F10** to Save your work so far – use the filename **Ex5b**. Do not print out at this stage.

14 You can edit the table using normal editing procedures if you notice any mistakes. Position the cursor in cell **C4** and change the size of the Eva Audio Case to **12" × 8"**.

Sorting the table items in a specified order

15 You are asked to modify the table layout so that the table items are rearranged to a specific order. You could simply key in the items in the order requested. Alternativcly you could use Cut and Move options to rearrange the blocks of text.

You can also *sort* the table items into a particular order using the standard sort commands. You must do this before you join (merge) any of the cells for the multi-line/column headings, or WordPerfect may display an error message. (Make sure you are *not* in Table Edit mode when you sort the table.)
To *sort* the table you have just keyed in into alphabetical order of STOCK DESCRIPTION:

```
Edit
Block
```

```
Tools
Sort
```

Position the cursor on the **Q** of **QW3**:
Press: **F12** or **Alt** + **F4** and shade all the text in the table.
Press: **Ctrl** + **F9**. The *Sort table* screen appears
Select: **3** (Keys)
Select: **a** (Alphanumeric) against **Type**
Enter: **2** against **Cell** (for the second cell in the table)
Select: **1** against **Line**
Select: **1** against **Word**
Press: **F7** to exit the keys option
Select: **1** (Perform Action)

The table items should now be sorted into alphabetical order of STOCK DESCRIPTION.

16 When you sort a table that has a mixture of double and single lines you will find that the lines become sorted along with the text, and sometimes the bottom line disappears altogether!

Press: **Alt** + **F7** (to go back into Table Edit mode)
Position cursor on the **C** of CAT REF NO
Press: **F12** or **Alt** + **F4** and shade the whole table
Select: **3** (Lines) **7** (All) **2** (Single)
Press: **F7** to exit Table Edit mode
Your table should now look as below:

CAT REF NO	STOCK DESCRIPTION	SIZE	COST[1]		P A G E
			-10	10+	
QW5	Eva Audio Case[2]	12" x 8"	7.99	6.99	4
QW7	Gem Audio Case	18" x 13"	9.99	8.99	1
QW8	Seva Audio Case	18" x 15"	6.99	5.99	3
QW3	Vax Audio Case	18" x 13"	9.99	7.99	2

1 Bulk orders of 50+ qualify for a further discount.

2 Available in black, red or green.

17 To join the cells for the multi-line/column headings: Press **Alt** + **F7** to go back into Table Edit mode. Position cursor in cell **A1** and press: **Alt** + **F4** or **F12**
Press: ↓ arrow key once – cells A1 and A2 are shaded in red
Press: **7** (Join) **Y** (Yes)

18 Repeat the last step to join cells **B1** + **B2**, **C1** + **C2** and **F1** + **F2** ('vertical joins'). Similarly, join cells **D1** + **E1** (a 'horizontal join').

19 Finally, there may be occasions when you will not be required to place horizontal lines above and below each item, but rather round a block of items. To do this: Press: **Alt** + **F7** to go into Table Edit (unless you are already in it)
Position cursor in cell **A3** (QW5)
Press: **F12** or **Alt** + **F4** and shade the rest of *column A only*, i.e. from *QW5* to *QW3*
Press: **7** (Join) **Y**(es)

Do not exit Table Edit mode yet.

Move to column B, and repeat the above procedure to join the items in column B. Repeat again for columns C, D, E and F.

Press: **F7** to exit Table Edit mode.

Important: if the text 'wraps' on to more than one line, you would not be able to use this method as the uneven lines would merge and become meaningless. As an alternative you could use the same procedure to shade each column, then choose the *lines* option and select *none*.

20 Position cursor at the top of your document above the table and centre the heading NEW RANGE OF AUDIO CASES
Check that your table now looks as Ex 5b in the print-out checks

21 *Save* and *print* a copy of your work – use the same filename **Ex5B**.

5.8 Exercise 5c.

Clear your screen. Key in your name and the task number on line 1. Enter the table shown below. The items should be rearranged in ascending order of *start time* for each *arena* number (follow the layout of the first three items) but keep the Junior and Adult Sections separate as displayed. Rule as shown.

For WordPerfect Version 5.0 – change the font to 12 pitch so the table will fit on A4 paper with the shorter edge at the top, without changing the margins. For WordPerfect 5.1 – change the font to 12 pitch *and* change the left and right margin settings to half an inch.

Save and *print* a copy of your work – use the filename **EX5C**.

SILSTON SUMMER FESTIVAL ← (centre)

EVENT TIME		DISPLAY TEAM	EVENT NAME	NAME OF ORGANISER	ARENA
START	END				
Junior Section					
1400	1430	JAY DANCEBIRDS	Sun & Wind¹	June Berry	1
1435	1500	FARRAH SINGERS	Junior Medley	Ann Shaw	1
1505	1525	JAY DANCEBIRDS	Dreams and Destinies	June Berry	1
1455	1525	FARRAH SINGERS	Southern Belle	Ann Shaw	~~2~~ 3
1505	1525	DANCE MINORS	Sugar & Spice	Maria Lee	2
1400	1500	FARRAH GYM SQUAD	Gymnastics	Mark Drew	2
1400	1445	SILSTON CHOIR	Yankee Doodle Dandy	Alan Green	3
Adult Section					
1530	1630	LAVELL DANCERS	Jazz American	Sue Vine	1
1645	1745	SILSTON Band	Bonanza Brass	Paul Knell	2
1630 ⤻	1530	SILSTON BAND	City lights	Paul Knell	3
1610	1630	THE DEVETTES	Guitar Duet²	Jo Devette	2
1645	1745	SILSTON CHOIRE	Showboat ~~Time~~	Alan Green	3
~~1530~~	~~1600~~	~~DANCE MAJORS~~	~~World Dance~~	~~Maria Lee~~	2
1530	1600	FARRAH SINGERS	ADULT Medley	Ann Shaw	2
1645	1745	SILSTON CHOIR	~~Hawaii~~ Copacabana	Alan Green	1

(please emphasise the words "Junior Section" and "Adult Section")

1 A mixture of classical ballet, jazz (and contemporary dance music) over the last century

2 Speciality act featuring Spanish Flamenco guitar & Spanish dancing by the Jay Dancebirds

General information

This is a method of combining (merging) data from two files into one file. The most common use of this feature is the production of 'personalised' letters. (An unpopular example of this is 'junk mail' – the same letter is sent out to many people, but printed with the individual's own name and address and other personal details.)

In WordPerfect the 'primary' file is the standard letter that is to be sent to many different addressees. The 'secondary' file is the data file containing the names and addresses (and sometimes other relevant data).

In the RSA Stage III Part 2 examination, you are required to key in:

1 a standard letter – the primary file

2 a data file of 10 addressees – the secondary file.

You will then select a particular cross-section (usually 6) of the addressees to receive the letter.

Finally, you will 'merge' the standard letter with the selected addressees from the data file and then print the letters.

Note: you are also required to produce print-outs of the standard letter and the *full* data file.

Creating your data file

The method varies according to the version of WordPerfect you are using, although the principle is the same. Each addressee will have a 'record' keyed in for him/her. Each record is made up of separate 'fields'. Look at the example below showing Mrs Waterston's record:

```
                                 Version 5.0   Version 5.1
Mrs P Waterston          )
12 Oak Drive             )
Netherton                )       ^F1^          {FIELD}    Name & Address Field
EDGERTON                 )
EN5 9OL                  )

Mrs Waterston            -       ^F2^          {FIELD}    Salutation Field

Veteran                  -       ^F3^          {FIELD}    Variable Data Field
```

The codes {^**F?**^ for Version 5.0 and (**FIELD**) for Version 5.1} shown in the example represent the codes as they will appear in the standard letter. For example, in Version 5.0 'Mrs Waterston' will be substituted for the code ^**F2**^ when the letter and data files are merged. In Version 5.1 the fields are identified at the top of the data file.

Each record should contain the same number of fields, and the fields should appear in the same order in each record.

Each field should always contain the same kind of information: in the example given Field 2 (the salutation field) must, of couse, actually contain the 'salutation' in every record.

In WordPerfect a code is inserted to show the end of each field and the end of each record. The code varies according to the version of WordPerfect you are using:

	Version 5.0	*Version 5.1*
End of field	^R	(END FIELD)
End of record	^E	^E

Mrs Waterston's record will therefore appear on screen as:

Version 5.0	Version 5.1
Mrs P Waterston	Mrs P Waterston
12 Oak Drive	12 Oak Drive
Netherton	Netherton
EDGERTON	EDGERTON
EN5 9OL^R	EN5 9OL{END FIELD}
Mrs Waterston^R	Mrs Waterston{END FIELD}
Veteran^E	Veteran{END RECORD}

Version 5.0

To insert an End of Field code {^R}

Press: **F9** immediately after last character

To insert an End of Record code {^E}

Press: **Ctrl** + **E**
(This method of inserting the ^E code is used in this book for the purposes of the RSA examination, as it allows the data file to be printed on two sheets of paper. If the ^E code is inserted by using the alternative command of **Shift** + **F9 E**, each record is printed on a separate sheet of paper. When you print out your data file for the examination, you may insert a hard page break between two of the records so that they are printed out sensibly, but you must remove this page break before you save the file for later merging.

Press: ↵ twice after completing each record *and* after the last record in the file.

Version 5.1

In this version the fields are defined at the top of the page before you key in the data. You can use names or numbers to define the fields that will be used in your data file and standard letter. It is suggested that the use of names may make your task easier.

To define the Field Names

```
Tools
Merge
More
{FIELD NAMES} ↵
```

Start with a clear screen

Press: **Shift** + **F9**
Press: **6** (More)
Press: **F** (Field)
Move cursor to: (**FIELD NAMES**) in box at top right of screen
Press: ↵
Type: **Name of first field** ↵ (e.g. address)
Type: **Name of second field** ↵ (e.g. salutation)
Type: **Name of third field** ↵ (e.g. variable)
(Repeat until all required fields are defined)

Press: ↵ again after all fields are defined.

Press: ↵ before keying-in first record

The top of your screen should now look like this:

```
{FIELD NAMES}address~salutation~variable~~{END RECORD}
================================================================
```

To insert an End of Field code {END FIELD}

Press: **F9** immediately after last character

```
Tools
Merge codes
More
{END FIELD}
```

To insert an End of Record code {^E}

Press: **Ctrl** + **E**

```
Tools
Merge codes
End Record
```

(This method of inserting the ^E code is used in this book for the purposes of the RSA examination, as it allows the data file to be printed on two sheets of paper. If the ^E code is inserted by using the alternative command of **Shift** + **F9 E**, each record is printed on a separate sheet of paper. When you print out your data file for the examination, you may insert a hard page break between two of the records so that they are printed out sensibly, but you must remove this page break before you save the file for later merging.

Press: ↵ twice after completing each record *and* after the last record in the file.

6.1 **Exercise 6a.**

To create your data file start with a clear screen. If you are using WordPerfect Version 5.1, first define the field names at the top of the page as explained previously. Enter Field 1 as: ADDRESS. Enter Field 2 as: SALUTATION. Enter Field 3 as: VARIABLE.
Key in the following name and address:

Mrs P Waterston
12 Oak Drive
Netherton
Edgerton
EN5 9OL

Immediately after the postcode insert an *end of field* code (**^R**) or {**FIELD**}. This marks the end of the address field or Field 1.

Note: the cursor jumps to the beginning of the next line – there is no need to press ↵

6.2 Key in **Mrs Waterston** (the salutation).

Insert another end of field code to mark the end of the salutation field or Field 2.

6.3 Key in **Veteran** (the variable data).

Insert an end of record code to show this is the end of Mrs Waterston's record.

6.4 Press ↵ twice and then key in the following four records to complete your data file, inserting end of field and end of record codes in the correct positions.

Don't forget to press ↵ twice after each record *and* after the last record in the file.

Mr I K Thompson 26 Summer Close Sunley LANGTON LN9 6EJ Mr Thompson Ordinary	Mr M E Willson 26 Fairway ROYDEN RN6 4JL Mr Willson Veteran	Mrs M Horsfall 18 Lea Rd Leafield BROOK HILL BK7 2HK Mrs Horsfall Veteran	Ms V Varley 4 Water Lane NORFIELD ND16 8LL Ms Varley Ordinary

6.5 Save your data file as DATA6A

6.6 *Version 5.0* – Print your data file DATA6A. (You may handwrite your name at the top of the data file printout after printing out if necessary.)

Version 5.1 – You will print your data file later – see step 6.20.

6.7 Clear your screen

Standard letter

The standard letter will contain merge codes to show where variable information is to be inserted during the merging procedure. Look at the example below.

```
Date

(^F1^ or (FIELD}address~)

Dear (^F2^ or (FIELD}salutation~)

As a (^F3^ or (FIELD}variable~) member of our Club, I
am writing to ask you if you would like to attend
our Annual Dinner to be held in two months' time.  I
attach full details and a tear-off slip.

Please return the completed slip as soon as possible
to be sure of a reservation.

Yours sincerely


M R Cheeseman
Chairman

Enc
```

To insert merge codes within a standard letter

Position cursor in required position.

```
Tools
Merge Codes
Field
(Type field name)
```

Press: **Shift** + **F9**
Type: **1** ← (Field)
Type: **Field number** (e.g. 1, 2, 3 ...) – *Version 5.0* or
Field name (e.g. address, salutation) – *Version 5.1*
(To indicate Field number or define the field content insert details as appropriate to the task in hand.)
Press: ↵
^F1^ appears on screen in Version 5.0.
{FIELD} name~ appears on screen in Version 5.1. When printing out the standard letter the {FIELD} part of the code is not printed, but name ~, address ~ etc. will be shown.

6.8 **Exercise 6a.** *continued.*

To create your standard letter key in **your name** and **Exercise 6A** on line 1.

6.9 Key in **today's date** on line 3 and press ↵ twice.

6.10 Insert a merge code for Field 1 (**^F1^** or **{FIELD} address~**) as previously described and then press ↵ twice again.

6.11 Key in **Dear** and then insert a merge code for Field 2 (**^F2^** or **{FIELD}** salutation). Press ↵ twice.

6.12 Key in the remainder of the letter as shown below inserting a merge code for Field 3 (**^F3^** or **{FIELD} variable~**) at the asterisk (*).

```
I am pleased to be able to tell you that the
event which has been organised for our spring
run is open to * members.  Please contact me if
you would like further details.

Yours sincerely


James Stevens
Events Organiser
```

6.13 Save your standard letter as **LETT6A**.

6.14 *Print* a copy of your standard letter.

Selecting the records to be merged

Start with a clear screen.

Tell WordPerfect which file you want to work on:

```
Tools
Sort
```

Press: **Ctrl** + **F9**
Press: **2** (Sort)
Type: **Datafilename** and press ↵ at 'Input file to sort:'
Press: ↵ at 'Output file for sort: (Screen)' (this will show your selected records on screen for you to check)

Tell WordPerfect what type of sort you want to perform:

Press: **7** (Type)
Press: **1** (Merge)

Give WordPerfect the 'key' for selecting records:

Press: **3** (Keys)
Press: **a** (Alphabetical) *or*
n (Numerical) depending on the type of data in the variable
Type: **3** (to select on Field 3) (or key in field number as appropriate to the task in hand)
Type: **1** (to select on line 1 of the field) (or key in line number as appropriate to the task in hand)
Type: **1** (to select on word 1 of line 1 of the field) (or key in word number as appropriate to the task in hand)
The field, line and word options identify the key word or number for selection. Take care when carrying out this procedure.

Press: **F7** (to Exit)

Tell WordPerfect the criterion for the variable 'key':

Press: **4** (Select)
Type: **key1=Veteran** ↵ ('Veteran' is an example of a variable)

Tell WordPerfect to perform a merge sort:

Press: **1** (Perform Action)

Your selected data records now appear on screen. Scroll through to check that they are correct.

Save your selected data using a different filename before you merge with your standard letter.

6.15 Exercise 6a. *continued.* To select the required addressees from your data file:

Starting with a clear screen, follow the instructions previously given to select all the records with the word *Veteran* as Field 3.

The input file to sort is: **DATA6A**.

6.16 Check that three records have been selected from the five that you inserted (for Mrs Horsfall, Mr Willson and Mrs Waterston).

If your selected records show any errors clear the screen without saving. Retrieve the standard letter and check that the merge codes are correct. Then retrieve the data file and check that the record codes are correct. Run the selection process again, checking the settings in the sort menu.

6.17 Save your selected records as **SORT6A** and clear the screen.

Merging and printing the data file with the standard letter

Starting with a clear screen:

Press: **Ctrl** + **F9**
Select: **1** (Merge)
Type: **Letterfilename** at *primary file*: and press ↵
Type: **Sortfilename** at *secondary file*: and press ↵

Your selected and merged letters now appear on screen.
Scroll through to check that the letters are correct.

Save your merged letters under a different filename before printing.

6.18 Exercise 6a. *continued.* To merge the selected records with the standard letter. Merge the data file and the standard letter as previously described:

The primary file is: **LETT6A**
The secondary file is: **SORT6A**
(The last letter shows on screen. Scroll up to view all the letters.)

Exercise 6a.
continued.

Printing one page of a multi-page document from the list files screen

Position the cursor on the file you want to print:

Press: **4** (Print)
Type: **1** (or number of the page you want to print) at (**All**)
Press: ↵

In the RSA Stage III Part 2 examination, you are required to print out all of the merged letters (usually six letters). However, while you are practising you might like to save paper by printing out only one letter for checking. If you are working with a tutor you could demonstrate that your mail merge has worked satisfactorily by having the file on screen.

6.19 *Save* your merged letters as **MERGE6A** and clear the screen.

6.20 *Print* one of your merged letters from the list files screen (filename is **MERGE6A**).

6.21 *Version 5.1* Print your data file. Retrieve your file: **DATA6A**

Delete the page break immediately below the FIELD NAMES information line as follows:

6.22 Place cursor on page 2, line 1, position 1 and press **← Del**. If necessary, press ↵ to separate the first record from the FIELD NAMES information line.

6.23 Save and print a copy of your data file. Use the same filename (**DATA6A**). (You may handwrite your name at the top of the data file printout after printing out if necessary.)

Selecting records using more than one criterion

In the RSA Stage III Part 2 examination, and in practice, it may be necessary for you to use two 'keys' when you are asking WordPerfect to select certain records from a data file.

For example, to select the three records with the criterion '4 April' from the list below, you would have to use the key '4' *and* the key 'April'.

3 April	13 April	4 November
4 April	4 March	14 April
21 June	25 June	27 April
4 April	4 July	4 April

To sort on the first criterion

At the sort secondary merge file screen:
Press: **3** (Keys)
Select: **a** or **n** (Alphabetical or Numerical)
Type: **field number**, **line number** and **word number**, as appropriate

To sort on the second criterion

Move cursor to key 2:
Select: **a** or **n** (Alphabetical or Numerical)
Type: **field number**, **line number** and **word number**, as appropriate
Press: **F7** (to Exit)

To insert key for selecting records

Press: **4** (Select)
Type: **criterion for selection** as appropriate e.g. **key1=4*key 2=April** (* = and)
Press: **1** (Perform Action)

Exercise 6b.

Key in the following records as a data file *as one long column. Print* one copy. *Save* as **DATA6B.** To complete this exercise, you will later save your sort file as: SORT6B and your merged file as: MERGE6B

Mrs J Brookner
36 Windsor Road
Wooldale
Huddersfield
HD7 8WB
Mrs Brookner
Jazz Adult

Mr O Kozlowski
147 Kirkstone Ave
Highley
Brighouse
HD6 2BE
Mr Kozlowski
Jazz Junior

Ms L Knight
Thorn View
Kirkwood
Huddersfield
HD3 9DH
Ms Knight
Jazz Junior

Mr P M Robinson
151 Meadow Grove
Kirkwood
Huddersfield
HD6 4HM
Mr Robinson
Creative Adult

Mr E Dale
125 Newton Hill
Brighouse
HD6 3ME
Mr Dale
Creative Junior

Ms R E Rise
14 Wykeham Rose
Keighley
BD22 5DD
Ms Rise
Creative Junior

Mr B Brown
10 Sandy Hill Lane
Sowerby Bridge
HX3 3PO
Mr Brown
Jazz Junior

Exercise 6b. *continued*

Exercise 6B – letter to be sent to all our Jazz Junior members only, telling them about the competition. Please use today's date, ragged right margin and print the required letters. Save your letter as LETT 6B.

*
*
*
* } address field (^F1^ or {FIELD}address~)

Dear * salutation field (^F2^ or {FIELD}salutation~)

NORTHERN / JAZZ DUO COMPETITION /JUNIOR

The annual competition wl take place / as usual at Milltown Civic ~~Hall~~ Centre on Sat 2 May.

For the past few years, we have ~~been~~ entered between 4 and six couples and, last yr, Gary Murphy & Anna Mayman, of our Club were winners in the Under-13 section.

As a regular attender at our * variable field (^F3^ or {FIELD}variable~) sessions, I wd like to invite you to enter the competition and I enclose an application form. Please complete & return this to me asap giving the name of yr proposed partner. Further details / info about our special competition training ~~sessions~~ classes can be obtained from Mary Steward.

Yrs scly

Michelle Woodman
MEMBERSHIP SEC

Enc

When selecting the records for Jazz Junior member only, the formula to input at 4 Select is: Key1 = Jazz * Key2 = Junior

Exercise 6c.

Exercise 6C. Create a datafile containing the following details. Save as DATA 6C and print a copy.

Mrs C Beaty
16 Tennyson Drive
BACKWOOD
BD4 7MA
Cathy
Branch 1 Personnel

Mr AL Brearley
Bridge End
BROWNSHAW
BW9 3AB
Adrian
Branch 1 Personnel

Mrs W Cawdwell
10 Dean Cottages
Deanshaw
HIGH WELLS
HS3 3NB
Wendy
Branch 2 Personnel

Mr A K Basu
6 Hill View Drive
Carr Hill
BROWNSHAW
BW3 4HA
Asoke
Branch 1 Personnel

Ms A Forder
18 Thomas St
Southwood
BACKWOOD
BD6 7LJ
Alison
Branch 3 Personnel

Miss L Lord
10 Overwood Ln
Overwood
LONSDALE
LE9 6SN
Lynda
Branch 1 Personnel

Miss S Hussain
29 Nelson Ave
Renshaw
RAWTON
RN6 8JL
Shahena
Branch 1 Accounts

Miss J L Stocks
Birch View
BACKWOOD
BD10 4LM
Jenny
Branch 1 Personnel

Mrs C Lefevre
16 Lindon Way
RAWTON
RN5 7LM
Claire
Branch 1 Purchasing

Mr H Fischer
16 Trafford Close
Mererale
HIGH WELLS
HS4 9LW
Helmut
Branch 1 Personnel

6.15 Exercise 6c. *continued.*

Letter to be sent to all *Branch 1 Personnel* staff. Use today's date and justified right margin. Change 'Head of Department' to 'Section Manager' throughout.

*
*
*
*
*

CAPS

Human Resource Management - Current Issues

Dear *

The Co is holding training ~~courses~~ sessions over the coming 6 months & I wd like to invite you to attend. I am writing to all staff employed in * ~~departments throughout our organisation~~. The sessions wl run for 2 or 3 days, depending on the content, and accom wl be provided. The following ~~venues~~ towns will be used: ✓

BIRMINGHAM
LEEDS
GLASGOW
ABERDEEN
NEWCASTLE
BRISTOL
LONDON
BELFAST

Please leave space for logo at left - to measure at least 3" across x 2" down - (75mm x 50mm)

Attendance wl be at the discretion of yr Head of Dept with whom you shd discuss yr interest. I enclose full details of the various courses & an application form. Please return yr form completed to your Head of Dept.

I look forward to seeing you at one of the above venues.

I hope you will ~~find~~ consider the proposed sessions ~~to be~~ relevant to yr day-to-day work. It is our policy to keep abreast of new developments in current ~~practise~~ practice & to apply new ideas in a practical way w. the complete involvement of staff at all levels.

Yrs sincerely

PERFECT BUILDING SOCIETY

M D TRAVIS
Personnel Director

Encs

Printing out arrangements in the RSA Stage III Part 2 examination

You are given 12 sheets of A4 paper in this examination. This is sufficient to be able to print out the following:

- one *draft* copy of the table
- one *final* copy of the table
- one *final* copy of the form
- one *final* copy of your data file (2 sheets)
- one *final* copy of your standard letter
- six *final* copies of the merged letters

You *will not* have sufficient paper to print a draft copy of any of the tasks, except the table. Use WordPerfect's *view* facility to make sure your documents are accurate before you save and print.

The printing of the final copies of the tasks in this examination is done outside the examination time of one-and-a-quarter hours *by the candidate.*

No amendments may be made to the text after that time has expired and, in WordPerfect, the printing is done from the list files screen. (*There is no need to retrieve the document to print.*)

You are allowed to insert special characters by hand, such as accents, on to the final copies after the examination time.

If you have used a method of ruling the *table* which produces *only horizontal lines* on the printer, you will draw in the vertical lines with a pen after printing this task.

Don't forget that the *mail merge* task requires you to print:

- the full data file
- the standard letter
- copies of the merged letter (usually 6)

The invigilator at your examination centre will explain the procedures to be followed for printing in that centre.

Form design

Exercise Con2a

Please prepare this application form. Include the following headings where appropriate and allow sufficient space for each item. Change the word 'trip(s)' to 'excursion(s)' wherever it occurs in this task and also in the next task, CON2b.

Save and *print* a copy of your work – use the filename **CON2A**.

Surname, Forenames Address, Date of Birth,
Payroll No, Department,
No of Adult Places Required
No of Child Places Required, Signed, Date

APPLICATION FORM ← (spaced caps)
Company Weekend Trip

(Leave a space here at least 2½" across by 2½" down (63 mm x 63 mm) for a company logo)

Trip A: PARIS ___
Trip B: AMSTERDAM ___
Trip C: VIENNA ___
(please tick choice required)

I apply for a total of ___ places for the above trip. I agree to abide by the company rules and regulations for the duration of the trip.

(put the section for Trips in bold)

Exercise Con2b

Prepare this table, using the paper with the shorter edge at the top. Rearrange the employee names in alphabetical order of *surname* within each section. Rule as shown. *Save* and *print* a copy of your work – use the filename **CON2B**.

COMPANY WEEKEND TRIP ← centre

The following personnel are to be included on the 3 co weekend trips. Coaches (for all excursions) will depart from Head Office on Friday 26 Sep at 1330 hrs, & return Monday 29 Sep at 2230 hrs

CODE	EMPLOYEE NAME	PAYROLL NUMBER	TICKETS REQUIRED		TOTAL COST £
			ADULT	CHILD	
Trip to Paris - £90[1]					
A	Alexandria Ferry	34112	4	1	405.00
A	Mark Goodwill	33441	2	34	360.00
A	Jonathan Kettle	22480	2	3	315
A	Elizabeth Brant	22563	2	2	270.00
Trip to Amsterdam - £110[2]					
~~B~~	~~Janet Benson~~	~~34356~~	~~2~~	~~2~~	~~352.00~~
B	Brian McIntosh	31889	0	3	330.00
B	Francesca Hollings	23235	2	0	220.00
B	Grahame Dilling	22672	2	1	286.00
Trip to Vienna - £135[3]					
C	Margaret Pendle	27610	2	0	270.00
C	Matthew Jay	39118	2	0	270.00
C	Susannah Wharfe	34447	2	2	540.00

1 Child discount 50% (same discount for OAPs)
2 Child discount 40 per cent
3 No discount available.

please emphasise the 3 section headings, "Trip to Paris..." etc

Exercise Con2c

Please set up and print a data file with these 10 records

Mrs P Grant
Grattan & Moore Ltd
12-15 Cornfield Street
BRADFORD
BD3 4NF
Mrs Grant
11 July – 15 July

Mr M Akram
Greaves Bros Ltd
Slade Street
HALIFAX
HX2 3ES
Mr Akram
11 August – 15 August

Mrs J Baines
Vale Components PLC
Vale Mill
DEWSBURY
WF10 5MP
Mrs Baines
11 July – 15 July

Mr S E Pedlipska
Pedlipska Plant Hire Ltd
Hollinwell Works
KEIGHLEY
BD22 1HP
Mr Pedlipska
21 July – 25 July

Miss K M Bo ton
Birkby Signs Ltd
Birkby Lane West
CLECKHEATON
CN9 6BD
Miss Bolton
11 July – 15 July

Ms Y Wigglesworth
Outwood Electrics Plc
Royd Mill
LIVERSEDGE
BD13 3RS
Ms Wigglesworth
11 July – 15 July

Mrs S Saddique
Long & James Ltd
16 Melbury Road
SOWERBY BRIDGE
HX3 1EL
Mrs Saddique
11 August – 15 August

Mr M N Neocleous
Hellenic Foods
Valley Business Park
BRIGHOUSE
HD5 2AU
Mr Neocleous
21 August – 25 August

Mr K Firth
Firth Kitchens Ltd
West Road Mill
HUDDERSFIELD
HD2 7SF
Mr Firth
11 July – 15 July

Mrs P A House
Newall Products Ltd
Paddock Ave
SKIPTON
BD30 4DD
Mrs House
11 July – 15 July

Exercise Con2c *continued.*

(Please send this letter to all the companies which are interested in the dates 11 July – 15 July. Use a ragged right margin.)

*
*
*
*
*

Dear *

(Northern News Weekend Breaks) — emphasise

Thank you for contacting me about our new excursions programme. [I note that you wd be interested in arranging a ~~weekend~~ break in Amsterdam for employees at your Co for the ~~weekend~~ dates of * , and I have pleasure in enclosing full details.

The Hotel ~~Excellente~~ Parador wl be our base for the weekend. [As you can see from the photograph, it is a large, modern hotel w a wide range of amenities. (Colour leaflets/are enclosed.)

(Allow a square here 2" x 2" for photo. (50 mm x 50 mm))

The cost per person wl be £210 and this includes travel (to) and from ~~Bradford~~ Leeds, accom on a bed & breakfast basis, and insurance. Parties of 12 and over attract the privilege of one free place for the ~~organiser~~ leader ✓ organiser.

Please ~~contact me by~~ telephone me asap if you wish to make a def reservation as demand is proving to be unexpectedly high.

Yours ffly
NORTHERN NEWS

M Hickson
Travel Manager

Encs

Exercise 1a

OPPORTUNITIES UNLIMITED
West End Business Park
BOROUGHTON
BR4 7RF

Tel No: (0537) 544432 Fax No (0537) 68754 VAT No 184 9956 32

Date of typing Name Exercise 1A

PRIVATE

Mrs A Bottomley
26 Hollings Way
BOROUGHTON
BB10 1WB

Dear Mrs Bottomley

'GOING IT ALONE' SEMINAR – SATURDAY *(correct date inserted for Saturday after next)*

Further to yesterday's telephone conversation, I would like to let you have more information on the above event which is aimed at providing prospective 'entrepreneurs' with the opportunity to acquire as much information as possible. At the seminar, you will be able to benefit from the knowledge and experience of local leaders of industry and business.

> At Opportunities Unlimited, we acknowledge the fact that setting up in business on your own is an enormous step to take and we aim to help the budding businessman or businesswoman through the early stages.

The day will begin at 9.30 am with a talk by our Director, followed by approximately one hour of presentations on current 'start-up' schemes. After coffee at 11.00 am, the participants will be invited to separate into small groups and to pool their ideas and experiences in considering what makes a successful business. The afternoon will be your chance to put your idea(s) to an advisor and to receive individual advice.

I enclose a map showing the location of our temporary accommodation, and a leaflet on the seminar. I have sent a copy of this letter to Ms P Farren, your colleague. I look forward to seeing you at the seminar.

Yours faithfully

E A Sutcliffe
Conference Organiser

Encs

Copy to Ms P Farren

Exercise 1b

VAT No 354 6632 76

GEORGE CARTER & SON
125 Seaview Road
HORNSEA HN3 5PK
Tel No 0924-447825 Fax No 0924-552389

Date of typing Name Exercise 1B

FOR THE ATTENTION OF THE HEALTH AND SAFETY OFFICER

Baxter, Green & Co
Yates Quay
EASTPORT
ET4 7GH

Dear Sirs

A GOOD PLACE TO WORK?

Thank you for contacting me recently in response to our newspaper advertisement.

The GOOD PLACE TO WORK? campaign began in (last month) of this year and has definitely received a good response, both from employers and employees. The project employs 3 full time workers, and approximately 3 part time assistants from the region are used at each venue to ensure information reaches local organisations.

Our campaign's mobile caravan will be in the Eastport area in (month after next) and, as you know, we are looking for a suitable site to locate the caravan. It is necessary for us to be in the business centre of a town with sufficient car parking space for people to be encouraged to visit the exhibition without inconvenience. Your SEAVIEW ROAD factory would appear to be ideal and I have written to your Managing Director, James Green, requesting permission to use your company's resources. I have sent him a copy of this letter.

I enclose a brochure giving information on the project and exhibition and hope to hear from you before (a week on Friday) so that arrangements can be finalised.

Yours faithfully

H HAMILTON
Project Leader

Enc

Copy to James Green, Managing Director, Baxter, Green & Co

Exercise 1c

VAT No 354 6632 76

GEORGE CARTER & SON
125 Seaview Road
HORNSEA HN3 5PK
Tel No 0924-447825 Fax No 0924-552389

Date of typing Name Exercise 1C

FOR THE ATTENTION OF THE HEALTH AND SAFETY OFFICER

Baxter, Green & Co
Yates Quay
EASTPORT
ET4 7GH

Dear Sirs

A GOOD PLACE TO WORK?

Thank you for contacting me recently in response to our newspaper advertisement.

The GOOD PLACE TO WORK? campaign began in (last month) of this year and has definitely received a good response, both from employers and employees. The project employs 3 full time workers, and approximately 3 part time assistants from the region are used at each venue to ensure information reaches local organisations.

Our campaign's mobile caravan will be in the Eastport area in (month after next) and, as you know, we are looking for a suitable site to locate the caravan. It is necessary for us to be in the business centre of a town with sufficient car parking space for people to be encouraged to visit the exhibition without inconvenience. Your SEAVIEW ROAD factory would appear to be ideal and I have written to your Managing Director, James Green, requesting permission to use your company's resources. I have sent him a copy of this letter.

It is very important that as many people as possible visit the exhibition in view of the fact that legislation is already in place. The European Community guidelines set out clear responsibilities for employers and employees alike and all managers/supervisors need to be made aware of the part they must play in assessing workstations.

It is, of course, no less vital that work practices are also examined with the aim of increasing efficiency and decreasing potential dangers and factors which might promote disease and discomfort.

Name Exercise 1C

We hope to dispel some myths by giving factual information and advice based on thorough research.

I enclose a brochure giving information on the project and exhibition and hope to hear from you before (a week on Friday) so that arrangements can be finalised.

Yours faithfully

H HAMILTON
Project Leader

Enc

Copy to James Green, Managing Director, Baxter, Green & Co

2

Exercise 2a

Name Exercise 2A

GOING IT ALONE SEMINAR

Saturday (correct date inserted)

Opportunities Unlimited are pleased to organise this Seminar for prospective business owners in the Boroughton area.

Our offices are to be relocated in the West End Business Park, where our new, purpose-built accommodation is nearing completion. In the meantime, we are fortunate that we have been allowed to use the premises of the Vendôme Hotel, High Street, for our Seminar.

The Seminar will be held in the ground floor function suite and the programme for the day has been organised as follows:

0900 HRS - INTRODUCTION

Neil Ross, Marketing Director of Opportunities Unlimited will outline the programme for the day and will introduce the speakers and representatives from local industry, business and commerce.

1000 HRS - START-UP SCHEMES

Presentations will be made by the High Street banks, the Small Business Advisory Service and the British Franchise Association.

Topics will include: capital, loans, share issues, government schemes and development boards.

1100 HRS - COFFEE

1115 HRS - WHAT MAKES AN ENTREPRENEUR?

With the aid of case histories, participants will be encouraged to discuss the viability of the respective businesses, types of business organisation, franchising, market research, and employment law. The leader of each group will advise on Income Tax, VAT and National Insurance. The aim is to make the participants more aware of the pitfalls and pleasures of self-employment.

Name Exercise 2A

1245 HRS - LUNCH IN 1ST FLOOR CARVERY

1400 HRS - CONSULTATION SESSIONS

The 'experts' will make themselves available for individual consultation. Every participant can put forward his or her idea and receive valuable assistance.

1600 HRS - PLENARY SESSION/PRIZE PRESENTATION

Neil Ross, Marketing Director, will present an award - 'Business Idea of the Day' - together with a cheque for £250 to the 'entrepreneur' with the most original (and viable) business proposal.

(The winner will be chosen by all the experts present at the Seminar.)

Exercise 2b

Name Exercise 2B

A G O O D P L A C E T O W O R K ?

An Exhibition for Office Workers

The Information Technology revolution has changed the way we work and brought many benefits - both from the employer's point of view and the employees' angle. Although there are no serious occupational dangers such as you might find in an engineering workshop or a foundry, the office does have its own risks.

Managers/Supervisors Do you know what your responsibilities are under EC legislation?

It will be your job to assess every workstation in your section/department. It's up to you to make sure EC recommendations are met.

Electronic Office Workers/VDU Operators Do you suffer from eye strain, aching shoulders, back pain, headaches? What can you do to make your working day more comfortable? How can your employer help?

VISIT THE GOOD PLACE TO WORK EXHIBITION

Help yourself to a better workplace

Name Exercise 2B

The exhibition will offer:

- Inter-active Video
- Slides
- Displays
- Professional Advice
- Quizzes, Questionnaires

LEARN ABOUT 3 AREAS OF INTEREST:

Health Eye problems, muscular strain, repetitive strain injury, VDUs and problems with pregnancy. Is it really the computer's fault? What can be done to alleviate stress, strain and worry?

Ergonomics Workstations, systems, the workplace environment. It's usually easy to change some aspects such as chairs, desks, and lighting but it's more difficult to change the way we think and work!

This is a very extensive topic - you'll be surprised what's involved.

Safety Electricity, radiation, chemicals. Expediency can lead to inadequate and dangerous practices in the use of electricity. There are many toxic chemicals in offices (but there's no risk provided due care is taken). We'll give you the facts about radiation from VDUs.

Exhibition opens at 1000 hrs Monday - Saturday and closes at 1800 hrs Monday - Friday. (Early close Saturday 1600 hrs.) Phone 071-124367 for exact location in your town - ask for Hamish Hamilton.

A GOOD PLACE TO WORK?

APPEARING SOON IN A CAR PARK NEAR YOU!

Exercise 3a

Name Exercise 3A

BUSINESS SEMINAR

G O I N G I T A L O N E S E M I N A R

Saturday (correct date inserted)

Opportunities Unlimited is pleased to organise this Seminar for prospective business owners in the Boroughton area.

The Seminar is the first of its kind in the area and should attract much publicity from the media. We are hoping to organise suitable press coverage, eg the local newspapers.

The required fee for the full day will be £75.00 including lunch.

The Seminar will be chaired by Adam Flynn, Marketing Director of Opportunities Unlimited.

REF: OU/SH

Name   Exercise 3A   BUSINESS SEMINAR

THE PROGRAMME FOR THE DAY HAS BEEN ORGANISED AS FOLLOWS:

0900 HRS - INTRODUCTION

Adam Flynn, Marketing Director of Opportunities Unlimited will outline the programme for the day. He will then introduce speakers and representatives from local industry, business and commerce including:

1	Mr Ahmed Khan	-	CHAIRMAN, Ridings & Holt Ltd
2	Mr Paul Knight	-	MANAGING DIRECTOR, Vernons & Hoyle Ltd
3	Mrs Vanessa Debarry	-	SOLICITOR, Mayes, Drew & Smithies
4	Ms Gladys Fairway	-	MANAGING DIRECTOR, Century Systems

1000 HRS - START-UP SCHEMES

Presentations will be made by the High Street banks, the Small Business Advisory Service and the British Franchise Association. Topics will include:

1 Capital

2 Loans

3 Development Boards

4 Government Schemes

5 Share Issues

6 Organisational Skills

There will also be a short talk from Mr Alan Stevenson who will advise on available help through various Government start-up schemes, eg financial assistance, administrational support etc.

1100 HRS - COFFEE

REF: OU/SH   2

Name   Exercise 3A   BUSINESS SEMINAR

1115 HRS - WHAT MAKES AN ENTREPRENEUR?

The speakers for each topic will lead a 45-minute debate on Income Tax, VAT and National Insurance. The aim is to make the participants more aware of the pitfalls and pleasures which come with self-employment.

With the aid of case histories, participants will be divided into groups and encouraged to discuss the viability of the respective businesses, types of business organisation, franchising, market research, and employment law.

The groups will then have an opportunity to put forward the main points from their discussions, including any particular questions which remain unanswered.

There will be a short 10-minute interval half-

way through this session.

1300 HRS - LUNCH IN 1ST FLOOR CARVERY

REF: OU/SH   3

Name   Exercise 3A   BUSINESS SEMINAR

<u>1400 HRS - CONSULTATION SESSIONS</u>

The 'experts' will make themselves available for individual consultation. Every participant can put forward his or her idea and receive, in return, valuable assistance along with constructive criticism.

There will be a short 10-minute interval half-

way through this session.

<u>1600 HRS - PLENARY SESSION/PRIZE PRESENTATION</u>

Adam Flynn, Marketing Director, will present an award - 'Business Idea of the Day' - together with a cheque for £175.00 to the 'entrepreneur' with the most original (and viable) business proposal.

(THE WINNER WILL BE CHOSEN BY THE PANEL OF EXPERTS

PRESENT AT THE SEMINAR.)

NB: Our offices are to be relocated in the West End Business Park, where our new, purpose-built accommodation is nearing completion. In the meantime, we are fortunate that we have been allowed to use the premises of the Stratton Hotel, High Street, for our Seminar.

REF: OU/SH   4

Exercise 3b

Name   Exercise 3B   EXHIBITION

A G O O D P L A C E T O W O R K ?

<u>An Exhibition for Office Workers</u>

The Information Technology revolution has changed our working lives and brought numerous benefits - both from the employer's point of view and the employees' angle. Although there are no serious occupational dangers (such as you might find in an engineering workshop or a foundry), there are still risks involved for those who work in an office environment.

<u>Managers/Supervisors</u>   Do you know <u>exactly</u> what your responsibilities are under European Community legislation?

New government laws are now in effect which regulate the number of hours an operator may sit at a VDU without a break.

It is your job to assess the safe working order of every workstation in your section/department. It's up to you to make sure European Community recommendations are met.

<u>Electronic Office Workers/VDU Operators</u>   If you suffer from eye strain, aching shoulders, back pain, headaches, you should ask the following questions:

1 What can you do to make your working day more comfortable?

2 How can your employer help?

3 Are you taking sufficient breaks away from the VDU screen?

4 Is the office furniture adequate, eg chair set to correct height and with a backrest?

5 Is the air-conditioning effective?

6 Have you had your eyesight checked by an optician since you started working on a VDU?

OFFICE WORKERS

Name Exercise 3B **EXHIBITION**

THERE WILL BE CONTINUOUS LECTURES ABOUT 3 AREAS OF INTEREST:

Health Eye problems, muscular strain, repetitive strain injury, VDUs and pregnancy. Are all health problems really the computer's fault? What can be done to alleviate stress, strain and worry?

Ergonomics Workstations, systems, the workplace environment. It's usually easy to change some aspects such as chairs, desks, and lighting but it's more difficult to change the way we work and think!

This is a very extensive topic - you will be surprised what is involved.

Safety Electricity, radiation, chemicals. Expediency can lead to inadequate and dangerous practices in the use of electricity. There are many toxic chemicals in offices (but there's no risk provided due care is taken - 95% of accidents are caused through negligence). We'll give you the facts about radiation from VDUs.

2 OFFICE WORKERS

Name Exercise 3B **EXHIBITION**

THE EXHIBITION WILL OFFER:

1 Inter-active Video

2 Slides

3 Displays from leading manufacturers

4 Professional Advice from the many experts who will be on hand to deal with your individual problems

5 Quizzes, Questionnaires

There will also be an Information Stand offering advice on European Community legislation.

3 OFFICE WORKERS

Consolidation 1

Name Exercise 3B

EXHIBITION

OPENING TIMES

Exhibition opens at 0930 hrs Monday - Saturday and closes at 1800 hrs Monday - Friday. (Early close Saturday 1600 hrs.) Phone 071-124637 for exact location in your town - ask for Hamish Hamilton.

Admission fee: £1.00 Adults
£0.50 Children (accompanied)
£0.50 OAPs

Parties of 10 or more qualify for a 10% discount.

A G O O D P L A C E T O W O R K ?

An Exhibition for Office Workers

APPEARING SOON NEAR YOU!

4 OFFICE WORKERS

Exercise Con1a

BURNDALE TERTIARY COLLEGE
Shaftesbury Road
BURNDALE
BE1 3WB

TEL NO (055) 375896
FAX NO (055) 623569

Date of typing Name Exercise CON1A

URGENT

Mrs U Adamson
Careers Teacher
Queen Anne's High School
Wellington Grove
BURNDALE
BE2 5AB

Dear Mrs Adamson

Visitors' Day

I am writing to tell you about next week's Visitors' Day at our College. Although it is rather short notice, I hope you will be able to attend, along with members of your staff and pupils. I must apologise for the letter's lateness; this is due to the fact that we have been waiting for the printing of our brochure and application forms, copies enclosed, to be completed.

The College will be open between the hours of 9 am and 7 pm on Thursday (next Thursday's date) and a buffet lunch will be served in the Training Restaurant for a limited number of careers teachers.

I am sending a copy of this letter to the Head of your 6th Form. Please return the enclosed form if you wish to join us for lunch - or telephone my secretary on Ext(ension) 3164 as soon as possible.

We believe the Visitors' Day is an excellent opportunity for school pupils to get the information they require and to experience a day in the working life of the College. Pupils can view the accommodation and receive help and advice in selecting a course to suit them. The College Admissions Department will be available to make separate appointments for those pupils who wish to make a definite commitment to a full time course.

Yours sincerely

M J CRABTREE
Marketing Officer, Burndale Tertiary College

Encs

Copy to Head of 6th Form, Queen Anne's High School

Exercise Con 1b

Name   Exercise Con1B

BURNDALE TERTIARY COLLEGE
Shaftesbury Road
BURNDALE   BE1 3WB

B U S I N E S S   A D M I N I S T R A T I O N

Full time Courses

Business Administration courses are related to National Vocational Qualifications (NVQs) at levels 2, 3 and 4. Students follow a programme based on their previous experience and qualifications, and designed to meet each individual's needs. All courses run for 1 year but may be extended to 2 years for those who wish to improve their job prospects and qualifications.

Our courses provide an excellent starting point for a career in the business world. The skills learned can be transferred to many different jobs at different levels - from office junior to managing director.

The Business Administration Programme

The core subjects are:

Typewriting
Word Processing
Computer Applications

The timetable is organized in such a way that students can then choose additional options from the following list:

Shorthand	Book-keeping
Audio-typewriting	European Studies
German for Business*	French for Business*
Desk Top Publishing	Statistics for Business*

* A GCSE grade A-C in the relevant language is necessary in order to begin studying languages for business and in mathematics for statistics for business.

Name   Exercise Con1B

Practical Experience

The majority of the work is practical in nature and students work at their own pace. Work placements are a valuable part of all our courses. Students work in local businesses for 3 weeks - 1 week per term in a 3-term course.

How to Apply

An application form may be completed at any time - not just during the Spring and Summer terms. It can be a definite advantage to apply early as the courses are popular. Forms should be received by the Admissions Officer, Jenny McEwan, by the end of June so that preliminary interviews can be organized. However, late applications are very welcome. It's never too late!

Commencement of Courses

The courses will begin on Monday 9 September at 9.00 am. Attendance is from 9.00 am to 5.00 pm each day except Wednesday when the afternoon is left free for leisure/creative pursuits.

COME TO OUR VISITORS' DAY

Thursday (correct date inserted)

9.00 am - 7.00 pm

Exercise Con1c

Name Exercise Con1C

BA/COURSES

BURNDALE TERTIARY COLLEGE
Shaftesbury Road
BURNDALE BE1 3WB

<u>COURSES IN BUSINESS ADMINISTRATION</u>

FULL-TIME COURSES

Business Administration courses are centred around National Vocational Qualifications (NVQs) at levels 2, 3 and 4. Students follow a 'modular' programme, the structure of which is based on their previous experience and qualifications. All courses run for 1 year from September - June but may be extended to 2 years for those who wish to improve their job prospects with advanced qualifications.

Our courses provide an excellent basis for a career in the world of business. The skills learned can be transferred to many different jobs at different levels - from Office Junior to Managing Director.

COME TO OUR VISITORS' DAY

<u>Thursday (correct date inserted)</u>

9.00 am - 7.00 pm

Name Exercise Con1C

BA/COURSES

THE BUSINESS ADMINISTRATION PROGRAMME

The core subjects are:

Typewriting	Office Administration
Word Processing	Computer Applications

The timetable is organised in such a way that students can then choose additional options from the following list:

Shorthand	Book-keeping
Audio-typewriting	European Studies
German for Business*	French for Business*
Desk Top Publishing	Statistics for Business*

* A GCSE grade A-C in German or French is necessary in order to begin studying the languages for business and in mathematics for 'Statistics for Business'.

PRACTICAL EXPERIENCE

The majority of the training is practical in nature and students work at their own pace. Work experience is a valuable part of all our courses. Students carry out 'real work' in local businesses for 3 weeks - 1 week per term in a 3-term course.

In the past, we have (wherever possible) organised a different work placement for each of the 3 weeks.

The College is proud of its technology, eg 3 rooms of new up-to-date computers, 2 colour laser printers and a range of industry-standard software packages.

PAGE NO 2

Name Exercise Con1C

BA/COURSES

PART-TIME COURSES

We offer a wide range of part-time courses either in single subjects (eg typewriting, word processing, shorthand) and also in Business Administration NVQ Levels 2 and 3. Some examples of these are listed below:

PAGE NO 3

Name Exercise Con1C

BA/COURSES

COMMENCEMENT OF COURSES

All full time courses commence on Monday 9 September at 9.00 am.

Enrolment dates for part time courses are available from the College Reception and are also published 2 weeks prior to commencement in the local press.

HOW TO APPLY

An application form may be completed at any time. It can be a definite advantage to apply early as the courses are popular. Application forms for full time courses should be received by the Admissions Officer, Jenny McEwan, by the end of June so that preliminary interviews can be organised. However, late applications are very welcome. It's never too late!

COME TO OUR VISITORS' DAY

<u>Thursday (correct date inserted)</u>

9.00 am – 7.00 pm

PAGE NO 4

Exercise 4a

Name Exercise 4A

J U N I O R   M E M B E R S H I P   F O R M

Jo-Jo Junior Dance Team

Membership No *

Surname *

First Name *

Address *

Tel No *

Age *

Date of Birth *

Sex *

Attending: JAZZ - Monday
MODERN DANCE - Wednesday
BALLET - Friday
CREATIVE DANCE - Saturday

(please tick sessions to be attended)

Fee Paid *

Date of Joining *

Exercise 4b

Name Exercise 4B

TELEPHONE MESSAGE

ACTION: URGENT/NON-URGENT
RING BACK
WILL CALL AGAIN LATER

MESSAGE FOR ....

DATE .... TIME ....

CALLER'S NAME ....

CALLER'S COMPANY ....

CALLER'S TEL NO ....

MESSAGE ....

....

....

....

Received by .... Date ....

(NB: line draw not mandatory)

Exercise 5b

Name Exercise 5b

NEW RANGE OF AUDIO CASES

CAT REF NO	STOCK DESCRIPTION	SIZE	COST[1]		PAGE
			-10	10+	
QW5	Eva Audio Case[2]	12" x 8"	7.99	6.99	4
QW7	Gem Audio Case	18" x 13"	9.99	8.99	1
QW8	Seva Audio Case	18" x 15"	6.99	5.99	3
QW3	Vax Audio Case	18" x 13"	9.99	7.99	2

1 Bulk orders of 50+ qualify for a further discount.

2 Available in black, red or green.

Exercise 5c

Name Exercise 5c

SILSTON SUMMER FESTIVAL

EVENT TIME		DISPLAY TEAM	EVENT NAME	NAME OF ORGANISER	ARENA
START	END				
JUNIOR SECTION					
1400	1430	JAY DANCEBIRDS	Sun and Wind[1]	June Berry	1
1435	1500	FARRAH SINGERS	Junior Medley	Ann Shaw	1
1505	1525	JAY DANCEBIRDS	Dreams and Destinies	June Berry	1
1400	1500	FARRAH GYM SQUAD	Gymnastics	Mark Drew	2
1505	1525	DANCE MINORS	Sugar and Spice	Maria Lee	2
1400	1445	SILSTON CHOIR	Yankee Doodle Dandy	Alan Green	3
1455	1525	FARRAH SINGERS	Southern Belle	Ann Shaw	3
ADULT SECTION					
1530	1630	LAVELL DANCERS	Jazz American	Sue Vine	1
1645	1745	SILSTON CHOIR	Copacabana	Alan Green	1
1530	1600	FARRAH SINGERS	Adult Medley	Ann Shaw	2
1610	1630	THE DEVETTES	Guitar Duet[2]	Jo Devette	2
1645	1745	SILSTON BAND	Brass Bonanza	Paul Knell	2
1530	1630	SILSTON BAND	City Lights	Paul Knell	3
1645	1745	SILSTON CHOIR	Showboat	Alan Green	3

1 A mixture of classical ballet, jazz and contemporary dance music over the last century

2 Speciality act featuring Spanish Flamenco guitar and Spanish dancing by the Jay Dancebirds

Exercise 6a

Name Exercise 6A (Data file)

address~salutation~variable~~

Mrs P Waterston
12 Oak Drive
Netherton
EDGERTON
EN5 9OL
Mrs Waterston
Veteran^E

Mr M E Willson
26 Fairway
ROYDEN
RN6 4JL
Mr Willson
Veteran^E

Mrs M Horsfall
18 Lea Road
Leafield
BROOK HILL
BK7 2HK
Mrs Horsfall
Veteran^E

Ms V Varley
4 Water Lane
NORFIELD
ND16 8LL
Ms Varley
Ordinary^E

Mr I K Thompson
26 Summer Close
Sunley
LANGTON
LN9 6EJ
Mr Thompson
Ordinary^E

Name Exercise 6A (Standard letter)

Today's date

^F1^ or address~

Dear **^F2^ or salutation~**

I am pleased to ber able to tell you that the event which has been organised for our spring run is open to **^F3^ or variable~** members. Please contact me if you would like further details.

Yours sincerely

James Stevens

Name   Exercise 6A   (Merged letters)

Today's date

Mrs M Horsfall
18 Lea Road
Leafield
BROOK HILL
BK7 2HK

Dear Mrs Horsfall

I am pleased to be able to tell you that the event which has been organised for our spring run is open to Veteran members. Please contact me if you would like further details.

Yours sincerely

James Stevens
Events Organiser

==

LETTERS ALSO TO: **Mrs P Waterston and Mr M E Willson**

Exercise 6b (NB: This file will appear as one column)

Name   Exercise 6B   (Date file)

address~salutation~variable~~

Mrs J Brookner
36 Windsor Road
Wooldale
HUDDERSFIELD
HD7 8WB
Mrs Brookner
Jazz Adult^E

Mr E Dale
125 Newton Hill
BRIGHOUSE
HD6 3ME
Mr Dale
Creative Junior^E

Mr O Kozlowski
147 Kirkstone Avenue
Highley
BRIGHOUSE
HD6 2BE
Mr Kozlowski
Jazz Junior^E

Ms R E Rose
14 Wykeham Rise
KEIGHLEY
BD22 5DD
Ms Rose
Creative Junior^E

Ms L Knight
Thorn View
Kirkwood
HUDDERSFIELD
HD6 9DH
Ms Knight
Jazz Junior^E

Mr B Brown
10 Sandy Hill Lane
SOWERBY BRIDGE
HX3 3PO
Mr Brown
Jazz Junior^E

Mr P M Robinson
151 Meadow Grove
Kirkwood
HUDDERSFIELD
HD6 4HM
Mr Robinson
Creative Adult^E

Name   Exercise 6B   (Standard letter)

(Date of typing)

^F1^ or address~

Dear **^F2^ or salutation~**

NORTHERN JUNIOR JAZZ DUO COMPETITION

The annual competition will take place as usual at Milltown Civic Centre on Saturday 2 May. For the past few years, we have entered between 4 and 6 couples and, last year, Gary Murphy and Anna Mayman of our Club were winners in the Under-13 section.

As a regular attender at our **^F3^ or variable~** sessions, I would like to invite you to enter the competition and I enclose an application form. Please complete and return this to me as soon as possible giving the name of your proposed partner.

Further information and details about our special competition training sessions can be obtained from Mary Steward.

Yours sincerely

Michelle Woodman
MEMBERSHIP SECRETARY

Enc

Name Exercise 6B (Merged letters)

(Date of typing)

Ms L Knight
Thorn View
Kirkwood
HUDDERSFIELD
HD6 9DH

Dear Ms Knight

NORTHERN JUNIOR JAZZ DUO COMPETITION

The annual competition will take place as usual at Milltown Civic Centre on Saturday 2 May. For the past few years, we have entered between 4 and 6 couples and, last year, Gary Murphy and Anna Mayman of our Club were winners in the Under-13 section.

As a regular attender at our Jazz Junior sessions, I would like to invite you to enter the competition and I enclose an application form. Please complete and return this to me as soon as possible giving the name of your proposed partner.

Further information and details about our special competition training sessions can be obtained from Mary Steward.

Yours sincerely

Michelle Woodman
MEMBERSHIP SECRETARY

Enc

==

LETTERS ALSO TO: **Mr B Brown and Mr O Kozlowski**

Exercise 6c (NB: This file will appear as one column)

Name Exercise 6C (Data file)

address~salutation~variable~~

Mrs C Beaty
16 Tennyson Drive
BACKWOOD
BD4 7MA
Cathy
Branch 1 Personnel^E

Mr A L Brearley
Bridge End
BROWNSHAW
BW9 3AB
Adrian
Branch 1 Personnel^E

Mrs W Cawdwell
10 Dean Cottages
Deanshaw
HIGH WELLS
HS3 3NB
Wendy
Branch 2 Personnel^E

Mr A K Basu
6 Hill View Drive
Carr Hill
BROWNSHAW
BW3 4HA
Asoke
Branch 1 Personnel^E

Ms A Forder
18 Thomas Street
Southwood
BACKWOOD
BD6 7LJ
Alison
Branch 3 Personnel^E

Miss L Lord
10 Overwood Lane
Overwood
LONSDALE
LE9 6SN
Lynda
Branch 1 Personnel^E

Miss S Hussain
29 Nelson Avenue
Renshaw
RAWTON
RN6 8JL
Shahena
Branch 1 Accounts^E

Miss J L Stocks
Birch View
BACKWOOD
BD10 4LM
Jenny
Branch 1 Personnel^E

Mrs C Lefevre
16 Lindon Way
RAWTON
RN5 7LM
Claire
Branch 1 Purchasing^E

Mr H Fischer
16 Trafford Close
Merevale
HIGH WELLS
HS4 9LW
Helmut
Branch 1 Personnel^E

Name Exercise 6C (Standard letter)

(Date of typing)

^F1^ or address~

Dear **^F2^ or salutation~**

HUMAN RESOURCE MANAGEMENT - CURRENT ISSUES

The Company is holding training sessions over the coming 6 months and I would like to invite you to attend. I am writing to all staff employed in **^F3^ or variable~** . I hope you will consider the proposed sessions relevant to your day-to-day work. It is our policy to keep abreast of new developments in current practice and to apply new ideas in a practical way with the complete involvement of staff at all levels.

The sessions will run for 2 or 3 days, depending on the content, and accommodation will be provided. The following venues will be used:

BIRMINGHAM
LEEDS
GLASGOW
ABERDEEN
NEWCASTLE
BRISTOL
LONDON
BELFAST

Attendance will be at the discretion of your Section Manager with whom you should discuss your interest. I enclose full details of the various courses and an application form. Please return your completed form to your Section Manager.

I look forward to seeing you at one of the above venues.

Yours sincerely
PERFECT BUILDING SOCIETY

M D TRAVIS
Personnel Director

Encs

Name Exercise 6C (Merged letters)

(Date of typing)

Mrs C Beaty
16 Tennyson Drive
BACKWOOD
BD4 7MA

Dear Cathy

HUMAN RESOURCE MANAGEMENT - CURRENT ISSUES

The Company is holding training sessions over the coming 6 months and I would like to invite you to attend. I am writing to all staff employed in Branch 1 Personnel. I hope you will consider the proposed sessions relevant to your day-to-day work. It is our policy to keep abreast of new developments in current practice and to apply new ideas in a practical way with the complete involvement of staff at all levels.

The sessions will run for 2 or 3 days, depending on the content, and accommodation will be provided. The following venues will be used:

BIRMINGHAM
LEEDS
GLASGOW
ABERDEEN
NEWCASTLE
BRISTOL
LONDON
BELFAST

Attendance will be at the discretion of your Section Manager with whom you should discuss your interest. I enclose full details of the various courses and an application form. Please return your completed form to your Section Manager.

I look forward to seeing you at one of the above venues.

Yours sincerely
PERFECT BUILDING SOCIETY

M D TRAVIS
Personnel Director

Encs

<u>LETTERS ALSO TO:</u> **Mr A L Brearley**, **Miss L Lord**, **Mr H Fischer**, **Mr A K Basu**, **Miss J L Stocks**

Consolidation 2

Exercise Con2a

Name Exercise Con2A

A P P L I C A T I O N F O R M

Company Weekend Excursion

Excursion A: PARIS .....

Excursion B: AMSTERDAM .....

Excursion C: VIENNA .....

(please tick choice required)

Surname ....

Forenames ....

Address ....

....

Date of Birth ....

Payroll No .... Department ....

No of Adult Places Required ....

No of Child Places Required ....

I apply for a total of .... places for the above excursion. I agree to abide by the company rules and regulations for the duration of the excursion.

Signed .... Date ....

Exercise Con2b

Name Exercise Con2B

COMPANY WEEKEND EXCURSION

The following personnel are to be included on the 3 company weekend excursions. Coaches for all excursions will depart from Head Office on Friday 26 September at 1330 hours, and return Monday 29 September at 2230 hours.

CODE	EMPLOYEE NAME	PAYROLL NUMBER	TICKETS REQUIRED		TOTAL COST £
			ADULT	CHILD	
EXCURSION TO PARIS - £90[1]					
A	Elizabeth Brant	22563	2	2	270.00
A	Alexandria Ferry	34112	4	1	405.00
A	Mark Goodwill	33441	2	4	360.00
A	Jonathan Kettle	22478	2	3	315.00
EXCURSION TO AMSTERDAM - £110[2]					
B	Grahame Dilling	22672	2	1	286.00
B	Francesca Hollins	23235	2	0	220.00
B	Brian McIntosh	31889	3	0	330.00
EXCURSION TO VIENNA - £135.00[3]					
C	Matthew Jay	39110	2	0	270.00
C	Margaret Pendle	27610	2	0	270.00
C	Susannah Wharfe	34447	2	2	540.00

1 Child discount 50% (same discount for OAPs)

2 Child discount 40%

3 No discount available.

Exercise Con2c

(NB: This file will appear as one column)

Name Exercise Con2C (Data file)

address~salutation~variable~~

Mrs P Grant
Grattan & Moore Ltd
12-15 Cornfield Street
BRADFORD
BD3 4NF
Mrs Grant
11 July - 15 July^E

Mr M Akram
Greaves Bros Ltd
Slade Street
HALIFAX
HX2 3ES
Mr Akram
11 August - 15 August^E

Mrs J S Baines
Vale Components PLC
Vale Mill
DEWSBURY
WF10 5MP
Mrs Baines
11 July - 15 July^E

Mr S E Pedlipska
Pedlipska Plant Hire Ltd
Hollinwell Works
KEIGHLEY
BD22 1HP
Mr Pedlipska
21 July - 25 July^E

Miss K M Bolton
Birkby Signs Ltd
Birkby Lane West
CLECKHEATON
CN9 6BD
Miss Bolton
11 July - 15 July^E

Ms Y Wigglesworth
Outwood Electrics PLC
Royd Mill
LIVERSEDGE
BD13 3RS
Ms Wigglesworth
11 July - 15 July^E

Mrs S Saddique
Long & James Ltd
16 Melbury Road
SOWERBY BRIDGE
HX3 1EL
Mrs Saddique
11 August - 15 August^E

Mr M N Neocleous
Hellenic Foods
Valley Business Park
BRIGHOUSE
HD5 2AU
Mr Neocleous
21 August - 25 August^E

Mr K Firth
Firth Kitchens Ltd
West Road Mill
HUDDERSFIELD
HD2 7SF
Mr Firth
11 July - 15 July^E

Mrs P A House
Newall Products Ltd
Paddock Avenue
SKIPTON
BD30 4DD
Mrs House
11 July - 15 July^E

Name Exercise Con2C (Standard letter)

(Date of typing)

^F1^ or address~

Dear **^F2^ or salutation~**

Northern News Weekend Breaks

Thank you for contacting me about our new excursions programme.

I note that you would be interested in arranging a break in Amsterdam for employees at your Company for the dates of **^F3^ or variable~** , and I have pleasure in enclosing full details.

The Hotel Parador will be our base for the weekend.

As you can see from the photograph, it is a large, modern hotel with a wide range of amenities. (Colour leaflets are enclosed.)

The cost per person will be £210 and this includes travel from and to Leeds, accommodation on a bed and breakfast basis, and insurance. Parties of 12 and over attract the privilege of one free place for the organiser.

Please telephone me as soon as possible if you wish to make a definite reservation as demand is proving to be unexpectedly high.

Yours faithfully
NORTHERN NEWS

M Hickson
Travel Manager

Encs

Name Exercise Con2C (Merged letters)

(Date of typing)

Mrs J S Baines
Vale Components PLC
Vale Mill
DEWSBURY
WF10 5MP

Dear Mrs Baines

<u>Northern News Weekend Breaks</u>

Thank you for contacting me about our new excursions programme.

I note that you would be interested in arranging a break in Amsterdam for employees at your Company for the dates of 11 July - 15 July, and I have pleasure in enclosing full details.

The Hotel Parador will be our base for the weekend.

As you can see from the photograph, it is a large, modern hotel with a wide range of amenities. (Colour leaflets are enclosed.)

The cost per person will be £210 and this includes travel from and to Leeds, accommodation on a bed and breakfast basis, and insurance. Parties of 12 and over attract the privilege of one free place for the organiser.

Please telephone me as soon as possible if you wish to make a definite reservation as demand is proving to be unexpectedly high.

Yours faithfully
NORTHERN NEWS

M Hickson
Travel Manager

Encs

<u>LETTERS ALSO TO:</u> **Mrs P Grant** **Miss K M Bolton**
Ms Y Wigglesworth **Mr K Firth**
Mrs P A House

OPPORTUNITIES UNLIMITED

West End Business Park
BOROUGHTON
BR4 7RF

Tel No: (0537) 544432 Fax No (0537) 68754 VAT No 184 9956 32

N.B. When using A4 sample letterheads mask out the letterhead which does not apply before photocopying.

GEORGE CARTER & SON
125 Seaview Road
HORNSEA HN3 5PK
Tel No 0924-447825 Fax No 0924-552389
AT No 354 6632 76

BURNDALE TERTIARY COLLEGE
Shaftesbury Road
BURNDALE
BE1 3WB

TEL NO (055) 375896
FAX NO (055) 623569

Accents (foreign words)

Before typing the character:
Press: **Ctrl + 2**
Type: **required letter**
Type: **required accent**

Allocate space

six clear lines = 1 in
10 characters = 1 in (10 pitch)
12 characters = 1 in (12 pitch)
Note: remember to change right margin to allocate space at right of document

Blocked capitals

Press: **caps lock key**

Bold text

Press: **F6** (to *start* bold)
Type: **text to be emboldened**
Press: **F6** again (to *end* bold)

Font / Appearance / Bold

To embolden text already keyed in

Press: **F12** or **Alt + F4**

Edit / Block

Shade area of text to be emboldened
Press:**F6**

Font / Appearance / Bold

To remove bold

See *Remove text emphasis*

Case, to switch upper and lower

Shade block of text to be changed with **F12** or **Alt + F4**

Edit / Block

Press: **Shift + F3**
Select: **1** (Upper case) or
2 (Lower case)

Edit / Convert / Case

Centre text

Press: **Shift + F6**
(cursor jumps to centre of line)
Type: **text to be centred**
Press: ↵ (text is centred)

Layout / Justify / Centre

To centre text already keyed in

Press: **F12** or **Alt + F4**

Edit / Block

Shade area of text to be centred
Press: **Shift + F6**
Answer **[Cntr]?Y/N** with **Y**(es)

Layout / Justify / Centre

To remove centring

See *Remove text emphasis*

To centre a page top to bottom

Press: **Shift + F8**
Select: **2** (Page) **1** (Centre Page) **Y**(es)

Layout / Page

Change logged drive

Press: **F5**
Type: = A: ↵ (or specify drive letter required)
Press: **F1**

Clear Screen

Press: **F7 N**(No) **N** (No)

Copy text

Press: **F12** or **Alt + F4**

Edit / Block

Shade area of text to be copied
Press: **Ctrl + F4**
Press: **1**(Block) **2** (Copy)

Edit / Copy

Position cursor where text is to be copied *to*
Press: ↵

Cursor movement

Around document

Press: ← → ↑ ↓

Word by word

Press: **Ctrl** + ← or **Ctrl** + →

Start/end of line

Press: Home + ← or Home + →

End of screen

Press: Home ↓

Start of screen

Press: Home ↑

End of document

Press: Home Home ↓

Start of document

Press: Home Home ↑

To move cursor to a specified page

Press: **Ctrl + Home**
Type: **no of page required** ↵

Date command

Press: **Shift + F5**

Tools / Date / Format

To set date format

Press: **3**
Type: **1 3 4** (i.e. format as 1 January 1994)

To insert date at cursor

Press: **1**

Tools / Date / Text

Delete a character

Move cursor to incorrect character
Press: **Del**
or
Move cursor to right of incorrect character
Press: ← (Del)

Delete to end of line

Press: **Ctrl + End**

Delete to end of sentence

Move cursor to start of sentence
Press: **F12** or **Alt + F4**
Press: **.** (full stop)
Press: **Del**
Type: **Y** (for Yes)

Edit / Select / Sentence / Delete

Delete to end of page

Press: **Ctrl + PgDn**
Press: **Y** (for Yes)

Edit / Select / Page / Delete

Delete a word

Move cursor to incorrect word
Press: **Ctrl** + ← (Del)

Delete a paragraph

Move cursor to beginning of paragraph or Block of text
Press: **F12** or **Alt + F4**
Shade area of text to delete
Press: **Del**
Type: **Y** (for Yes)

Edit / Select / Paragraph / Delete

Enter points

To set up

Use a suitable symbol for the enter point which doesn't normally appear in the text, e.g. $ or @

To search for

Operate *Search* command (**F2**) to locate the enter point. Delete it, then replace with appropriate information.
(Use *Typeover* mode if there is more than one enter point on the line.)
Note: remember to align enter points with a tab setting for information going on to more than one line.

Search
Forward

Exit WordPerfect

Press: **F7**
Type: **Y**(Yes) or **N** (No)
(to save file before exiting)
Type: **Y** (to exit)

File
Exit

Flush right text

Press: **Alt + F6**
(cursor jumps to right margin)
Type: **text to be right aligned**
Press: ↵

Layout
Justify
Right

Font to change size or appearance

Press: **Ctrl + F8**
Select: **1** (Size) or **2** (Appearance)
Select: from the options displayed

Font
Size or
Appearanc

To change back to normal font

Press: **Ctrl + F8**
Select: **3** (Normal)

Font
Normal

To change font of text already keyed in

First, block with **F12** or **Alt + F4**
Carry out font change as above

Edit
Block

Footers

Position cursor at top of document, but after any header command
Press: **Shift + F8** (Format menu)
Select: **2** (Page) **4** (Footer)
1 (Footer A)
Select: **2** (Every Page) (or choose another option)
Type: **the footer text**
Press: **F7** (exit footer screen)

Layout
Page

Footer with automatic page numbering

Repeat as for entering a footer, but after entering the footer text (e.g. page no):
Press: **Ctrl + B** (**^B**)
Note: text is not vital, **^B** can be used alone

Footnotes

Manual method

Use asterisk(s) e.g. * ** *** or **superscripted number** (3) to enter footnote(s) in body of text (no space before footnote symbol)
Leave one space after explanatory footnote symbol(s) at bottom of passage/document

Wordperfect method

Position cursor next to text requiring footnote
Press: **Ctrl + F7**
Select: **1**(Footnote) **1** (Create)
Press: **space bar** or **F4** Indent key
Type: **the explanatory footnote text**
Press: **F7** (Exit)

Layout
Footnote
Create

To edit footnote

Press: **Ctrl + F7**
Select: **1** (Footnote) **2** (Edit)
Key in footnote number to be edited
Make necessary changes
Press: **F7** (Exit)

Layout
Footnote
Edit

To delete the footnote

Position cursor on footnote number
Press: **Del Y**(es)

To move footnote

Delete footnote. Move cursor to new position
Press: **F1** (Cancel) **1** (Restore)

Edit
Move
Paste

To change footnote display

Press: **Ctrl + F7**
Select: **1** (Footnote) **4** (Options)
Select from the options shown and enter your requirements
Press: **F7** (Exit)

Layout
Footnote
Options

Fractions

To type a half ($\frac{1}{2}$)

Press: **Alt + 171** (use numbers on numeric keypad)

To type a quarter ($\frac{1}{4}$)

Press: **Alt + 172** (use numbers on numeric keypad)

Graphics line

Press: **Alt + F9**
Select: **5** (Line)
Select: **1** (Horizontal line) or
2 (Vertical line)
Select from the options given to alter line position, length, width, shading etc.
Press: **F7** (Exit)

Graphics
Line
Create
Horizonta
l
Create

Headers

Position cursor at top of document
Press: **Shift + F8** (Format menu)
Select: **2** (Page) **3** (Headers)
1 (Header A)
Select: **2** (Every Page) (or choose another option)
Type: **the header text**
Press: **F7** (exit header screen)

Layout
Page

Help

For information on any of WordPerfect's functions
Press: **F3** (the Help key)
Press: **the first letter of the feature you require information on**
or
Press: **F3** again (to display the help template)
Press: **the feature function key for additional information**
Press: **space bar** or ↵ to exit help

Help

Insert text

Simply type in character(s) at the appropriate place (making sure typeover mode is not in use)

Inset/indent key

Press: **F4** (to indent at left margin only)
Press: **Shift + F4** (to indent at left *and* right margins)
Note: Each time you press **F4** you indent by five spaces – press once to indent $\frac{1}{2}$ in – press twice to indent 1 in etc.

Layout
Align
Indent →
or
Indent

Justification on/off

Press: **Shift + F8**
Select: **1** (Line) **3** (Justification)
Version 5.0
Type: **Y** (Yes) or **N** (No)
Version 5.1
Type: **4** (Full) or **1** (Left)

`Layout / Line / Justify / Full`

Line draw

Press: **Ctrl + F3**
Select: **2** (Line Draw)
Select: **1**,**2** or **3** (type of line) or
Select: **4** (Change) and choose from one of the options displayed
Press: arrow keys to draw line in a given direction
Select: **6** (to move cursor without drawing a line, i.e. to re-position)
Select: **5** (to erase any unwanted lines)
Note: use **Typeover** mode to enter text into a drawn box

`Tools / Line Draw`

Line length, to alter

When using 10 pitch, 82 characters will fit on an A4 page. With default margins of 1 in, the line length is reduced to 62 characters

To alter the line length to a specified setting, either add or subtract to the margin settings as appropriate (e.g. to set a line length of 52 you could change both margins to 15)

Mail merge

See Unit 6 for a full explanation of how to operate a mail merge

Margins (to change)

Press: **Shift + F8**
Select: **1** (Line) **7** (Margins)
Enter new left/right margin settings
Press: ↵ twice (to get back to document)

`Layout / Line`

Marking files on List Files directory

From the List Files screen, position cursor on filename
Type: *
To mark all files
Press: **Home** *
To remove markers repeat procedure

Move block of text

Press: **F12** or **Alt + F4**
Shade area of text to be moved
Press: **Ctrl + F4**
Press: **1** (Block) **1** (Move)
Position cursor where text is to be moved
Press: ↵

`Edit / Block`
`Edit / Move`

New page marker

Press: **Ctrl** + ↵
To delete a new page marker use reveal codes to position cursor on the code and press **Del**.

`Layout / Align / Hard / Page`

Page numbering

Position cursor at top of document, but after any header code
Press: **Shift + F8** (Format menu)
Select: **2** (Page)
Version 5.0
Select: **7** (Page Numbering)
Version 5.1
Select: **6** (Page Numbering)
4 (Page Numbering position)
Select: **the number position required**
Press: **F7** (Exit)
Press: **F7** (Exit)

`Layout / Page`

Suppress page numbering on current page

After selecting the number position:
Version 5.0
Select: **9** (Suppress this page only)
Version 5.1
Select: **8**
Select: **4** (Suppress Page Numbering)
Type: **Y** (for Yes)
Press: **F7** (Exit)

Paragraphs

To make

Move cursor to first letter of new paragraph
Press: ↵ twice

To join

Move cursor to start of paragraph 2
Press: ← (Del) twice

Pitch, to change

Position cursor at top of document
Press: **Ctrl + F8**
Select: **4** (Base Font)
Select: **the required pitch**
(e.g. 12 CPI) by highlighting with cursor and pressing **1** (Select)

`Font / Base Font`

Print

Full document

Press: **Shift + F7**
Press: **1** (Full Document)

`File / Print`

One page

Position cursor on page to be printed
Press: **Shift + F7**
Press: **2** (Page)

`File / Print`

Print from List Files screen

Press: **F5** ↵ to bring up the List Files directory screen
Move cursor to highlight the file to print
Press: **4** (Print)
Press: **A**(ll) to print all pages in file or key in number of page(s) to be printed (e.g. **3** to print page 3 only)

`File / List Files`

Quick copy/move/delete

Position cursor anywhere within the text to be copied/moved/deleted
Press: **Ctrl + F4**
Select: **1** (for Sentence) or
2 (for Paragraph) or
3 (for Page)

`Edit / Select / Sentence / Paragraph / Page`

Press: **1** (Move) or
2 (Copy) or
3 (Delete)

Remove text emphasis

Press: **F11** or **Alt + F3** [Edit Reveal Codes]
Using arrow keys to move cursor, shade the code to be deleted (e.g. [**BOLD**], [**UND**], [**CNTR**])
Press: **Del** key
Press: **F11** or **Alt + F3** again [Edit Reveal Codes]
(to return to document)

Repeat characters

Press: **Esc**
Type: **No of repeats needed**
Type: **Character to be repeated**

Replace text – typeover

Move cursor to incorrect entry
Press: **Ins** key (typeover *on*)
Overtype with correct entry
Press: **Ins** key again (typeover *off*)

Restore deleted text

Press: **F1** (Cancel key) [Edit Undelete]
Press: **1** (Restore last deletion) or
Press: **2** (Restore next to last deletion)

Retrieve a file

Press: **F5** ↵ [File List Files]
(check you are on the right drive)
Select: **filename**
(use arrow keys to shade)
Press: **1** (Retrieve)
Y (Yes - if you are retrieving into your current file)
or
Press: **F10** [File Retrieve]
Type: **filename** ↵

Ruled lines

a) Version 5.1 – use 'Table' facility
b) Version 5.0 – use underscore for horizontal lines and rule vertical lines in black pen. Use **F1** to restore (repeat) horizontal lines.
c) use Line Draw facility
d) use Graphics Line

Save text and continue

Press: **F10** [File Save]
Enter **your filename**
Note: type **Y**(Yes) if you want to *replace* a previous file with the same name

Save text and exit

Press: **F7** [File Save]
Type: **Y** (to save document)
Enter: **your filename**
Press: **Y** (to exit the program)

Search for text

Press: **F2** (search forwards) or [Search Forwards]
Shift + F2 (search backwards) [Search Backwards]
Key in text to search for
Press: **F2** (to begin search)
WordPerfect will search through the document and stop on the first occurrence of the 'search'
Press: **F2** again to continue the search [Search Next]

Search and replace

Position cursor at top of document
Press: **Alt + F2** [Search Replace]
Press: **Y**(es) to confirm each replacement
or **N**(o) to replace without confirmation
Type the text (or enter the code) to be searched for
Press: **F2**
Type the replacement text (or replacement code)
Press: **F2**
Confirm where appropriate with **Y**(es)
'**Not found**' indicates end of search
Note: when searching/replacing a 'code' simply press the appropriate function key.

Search and replace 'beep'

To set a warning 'beep' for end of search
Press: **Shift + F1** (Set-up) [File Setup Environment]
Version 5.0
Press: **5** (Initial Settings)
Press: **5** (Environment)
Version 5.1
Press: **3** (Environment)
Select: **Beep Options**
Press: **3** (Beep on Search Failure)
Press: **Y** (for Yes)
Press: **F7** (to exit this menu)

Sort, by line

Press: **F12** or **Alt + F4** and [Edit Block]
shade the portion of text to be sorted
Press: **Ctrl + F9** [Tools Sort]
Select: **3** (Keys)
Select: **a**(lphanumeric) or **n**(umeric) to determine the type of sort
Enter: **the field number of your first sort key** (or press ↵ to accept 1)
Enter: **the word in the field to sort on** – **1**,**2**,**3**, etc. (or press ↵ to accept 1)
Press: **F7** (exit definition area)
Press: **1** (Perform Action)

To sort in descending order

Repeat above procedure, but before pressing 1 perform action:
Select: **6** (Order) **2** (Descending)

Spaced capitals

Press: **caps lock** key
Leave *one space between each letter*
Leave *three spaces between each word*

Spellcheck

Press: **Ctrl + F2** [Tools Spell]
Select: **1 Word** (check word)
2 Page (check page)
3 Document (check document)
Select: **4 New sup. dictionary** (if the word is not already in WordPerfect's dictionary and you wish to add it in)
Select: **5 Look up** (to check a spelling you are not sure of e.g. typing cons* ↵ will bring up any word with the sequence cons)
Select: **Skip once** (to skip the word the first time it occurs but stop on it whenever it occurs again)
Skip (to skip the word on every occurrence)
Edit (to return to document and amend the error,

then Press: **F7** to exit back to Speller)
Press: '**A**' (or the appropriate letter to select a correct spelling)
Press: **F7** (to return to document)

To spellcheck a block of text

Press: **F12** or **Alt + F4** and shade the area of text to be checked	Edit Block
Press: **Ctrl + F2** Continue with speller as normal	Tools Spell

Standard paragraphs

Position cursor where you wish to insert the text
Retrieve the file
(see methods described under this heading)
Press: **PgDn** to go quickly to end of retrieved text.

Superscript/subscript

Press: **Ctrl + F8** Select: **1** (Size) Select: **1** (Superscript) or **2** (Subscript)	Font Superscript Subscript

Table mode (Version 5.1 only)

To create a new table Press: **Alt + F7** Select: **2** (Tables) **1** (Create)	Layout Tables Create

Enter required number of columns and rows
Select from any of the Table Menu options on screen to create the desired table layout (see Unit 5 for a full explanation of table commands)
Press: **F7** (to exit Table Mode)

To edit a table

If your cursor is already inside the table
Press: **Alt + F7**

If your cursor is not inside the table Press: **Alt + F7** Select: **2** (Tables) **2** (Edit)	Layout Tables Edit

Select from any of the Table Menu options on screen to edit the table layout as appropriate
Press: **F7** (to exit Table Mode)

To delete a table

Press: **F11** or **Alt + F3** (Reveal Codes)	Edit Reveal codes

Using arrow keys to move cursor,
shade the table code to be deleted (e.g. [Tbl Def: I])
Press: **Del**

Press: **F11** or **Alt + F3** again (to return to document)	Edit Reveal codes

To sort a table

Please refer to Unit 5

Tabulation

Default tabs

Press: **Tab** key
(to move cursor to defaulted tabs already pre-set every five spaces)

To alter tab settings at tab menu

Press: **Shift + F8** Select: **1** (Line) **8** (Tab Set)	Layout Line

To clear all tabs

Type: **0** (zero) (not necessary in Version 5.1)
Press: **Ctrl + End** key once
(All the 'Ls' (tab stops) should disappear)
Note: this is known as 'delete EOL'
(Delete to End Of Line)

To delete one tab

Position cursor on tab to be deleted
Press: **Del** key

To set a tab

Position cursor on ruler line where tab is to be inserted
Press: **L** (left justified tab)
R (right justified tab)
C (centred tab)
D (decimal tab)
. + L or **. + R** (to display leader dots with a left or right tab setting)

To set tabs at regular intervals

Clear all tabs
Type: **0,5** (to set tabs every five spaces)
0,10 (to set tabs every ten spaces)

To exit tab menu

Press: **F7** twice
(to exit tab menu and return to document)
Note: pressing any other key,
e.g. **F1** or **Esc** or ↵ will *not* save the changes

Underline text

Press: **F8** (to *start* underline) Type: **text to be underlined** Press: **F8** again (to *end* underline)	Font Appearance Underline

To underline text already keyed in

Press: **F12** or **Alt + F4**
Shade area of text to be underlined

Press: **F8**	Font Appearance Underline

To remove underline

See *remove text emphasis*

Vertical headings

Enter the heading one character per line, e.g.
d
o
w
n

View document

Press: **Shift + F7** Press: **6** (View Document)	File Print

Select from options shown to see enlarged or reduced view of text
Press: **F7** to return to document
Note: use this option to view headers, footers, justification, footnotes, etc.

View file directory

Press: **F5** ↵ (List Files)	File List Files

Widow/orphan protection

Position cursor at top of document

Press: **Shift + F8** (Format menu) Select: **1** (Line) **9** (**W/O** protection)	Layout Line

Type: **Y** (for Yes)
Press: **F7** (Exit)

Important!

In WordPerfect there is no single 'panic' key (the key to press to go back a step or get you out of an option you selected by mistake)

Generally, in order to:

Cancel a command	Press: **F1**
Exit a 'menu'	Press: **F7**